AMID PERSECUTIONS

THE CHURCH GREW STRONG

LESLIE M. JOHN

AMID PERSECUTIONS

THE CHURCH GREW STRONG

LESLIE M. JOHN

Copyright ©1997-2015 Leslie M. John: All rights reserved

No part of this book may be reproduced or transmitted in any form or by any means, electronic or mechanical, including photocopying, recording, or by any information storage and retrieval system, without permission in writing from the copyright owner, Leslie M. John.

The entire text of this book and graphics are deposited with Library of Congress Copyright Office, 101 Independence Avenue, SE Washington, DC 20559-6000, USA. This work is protected by Law in US; and internationally, according to The Berne Convention 1971

Description: Keeping in view the various forms of persecutions not only of Christians of New Testament period, but also of those who suffered during Old Testament period, this book is written to encourage believers with the words of Lord Jesus Christ, who said "And fear not them which kill the body, but are not able to kill the soul: but rather fear him which is able to destroy both soul and body in hell" (Matthew 10:28)

Persecutions, in the lives of Christians, are a part of life and God does not promise to remove the persecutions from our lives but promises to deliver from them.

Persecutions may be of lesser intensity, like inflicting constant fear in the minds of people, or trying to subjugating them, or may be of extreme measure like slaying. In spite of the indisputable fact that the world has witnessed persecutions of Christians in various forms, it is also true that the Church grew in the midst of persecutions.

Jesus said "Blessed are they which are persecuted for righteousness' sake: for theirs is the kingdom of heaven" (Matthew 5:10)

In the light of the clear consolation Lord Jesus Christ gave that a Christian does not need to fear persecutions, but fear the one who is able to destroy soul and body, a believer does not need to fear persecutors in order to compromise the truth. No man can destroy the soul of a believer however intense persecutions may be. All that a man, who persecutes, can do is to destroy the fleshly body of the persecuted ones; and never the inner man of the believer.

Fear the Lord, who can destroy not only body but the soul of a person.

ISBN-10:0990780171
ISBN-13:978-0-9907801-7-5

PREFACE

My mission is to proclaim the good news of our Lord Jesus Christ as revealed to me through Holy Bible and from various teachers, preachers, and commentators. This is my voluntary service to God in the name of His only begotten Son Lord Jesus Christ.

I share the truth of knowledge of God with others with good intention of bringing them to the knowledge of the living God, the God of Abraham, the God of Isaac, the God of Jacob, and the Father of our Lord Jesus Christ. My mission is to proclaim the Gospel of Lord Jesus Christ and not converting forcibly anyone to Christianity.

There are fundamental Christian doctrines that I believe in and I will not compromise on those doctrines. They are:

God is Triune: The Father, The Son and The Holy Spirit. They are not three Gods, but One God in three persons, co-equal-co-existent and functionally different.

There is no salvation except by Grace through Faith in Lord Jesus Christ. I believe in:

"That if thou shalt confess with thy mouth the Lord Jesus, and shalt believe in thine heart that God hath raised him from the dead, thou shalt be saved" (Romans 10:9)

One may accept or reject any or part of my writings/teachings. No offense is meant to any individual or any religion or any organization.

I pray for the peace of Jerusalem and desire that all Jews may accept Lord Jesus as their personal Savior and Messiah.

"Pray for the peace of Jerusalem: they shall prosper that love thee" (Psalms 122:6)

I firmly believe in the saying of Jesus, who said:

"No man can come to me, except the Father which hath sent me draw him: and I will raise him up at the last day" John 6:44.

My efforts to teach or preach are of no use unless Lord Jesus Christ Himself intervenes and the Father draws a person unto Him.

All Scriptures in electronic format are from King James Version (KJV) from Open domain, and English Standard Version (ESV) The Holy Bible, English Standard Version Copyright © 2001 by Crossway Bibles, a division of Good News Publishers

CONTENTS

AMID PERSECUTIONS 1

PREFACE 5

SECTION I THE PERSECUTIONS 11

CHAPTER 1 PERSECUTIONS 13

CHAPTER 2 DISPUTE WITH PHARISEES.....................................17

CHAPTER 3 THE TRUTH SHALL MAKE YOU FREE 21

CHAPTER 4 EVIL BEGETS EVIL 24

CHAPTER 5 NABOTH'S VINEYARD 26

CHAPTER 6 GOD HATES IDOLATRY..29

CHAPTER 7 THE CHALLENGE 31

CHAPTER 8 ELIJAH CALLS FIRE FROM HEAVEN 36

CHAPTER 9 GOD SPOKE IN SMALL STILL VOICE 41

CHAPTER 10 JEZEBEL'S DEATH 44

CHAPTER 11 PERSECUTIONS IN THE NEW TESTAMENT.............46

CHAPTER 12 THE FIRST PERSECUTION 48

    PETER AND JOHN THREATENED..48

    HEALING OF LAME MAN 53

    IN THE NAME OF JESUS..55

    MIRACLES 58

    MIRACLES DO HAPPEN...61

    PRAISE AND WORSHIP 64

    KISS THE SON 65

    THE LESSONS..68

AMID PERSECUTIONS

CHAPTER 13 THE SECOND PERSECUTION 73
   ANANIAS AND SAPPHIRA 73
   APOSTLES ARRESTED 75
   ANGEL OF THE LORD RESCUES 76
   APOSTLES RESIST THE COUNCIL 77
   GAMALIEL CITES THEUDAS AND JUDAS 78

CHAPTER 14 THE THIRD PERSECUTION 79
   STEPHEN STANDS FOR JESUS 79
   STEPHEN GLORIFIES GOD 82

CHAPTER 15 THE FOURTH PERSECUTION 85
   SAUL PERSECUTES THE CHURCH 85
   APOSTLE PAUL TURNS TO GENTILES 87

CHAPTER 16 THE FIFTH PERSECUTION 93
   PETER RESCUED 93
   RHODA'S BELIEF 94
   PRAYER ANSWERED 95
   SOLDIERS EXECUTED 96
   HEROD KILLED 97
   THE CHURCH GREW 97

CHAPTER 17 VENGEANCE BELONGS TO GOD 98

CHAPTER 18 VENGEANCE IS NOT TOO FAR 101

CHAPTER 19 PAUL'S BOLDNESS 104

CHAPTER 20 PAUL TURNS TO GENTILES 107

CHAPTER 21 FOLLOW JESUS: NO EXCUSES 112

CHAPTER 22 PAUL AND PERSECUTIONS	115
SECTION II THE CHURCH GREW STRONG	118
CHAPTER 23 THE ONE NEW MAN	119
THE FIRST CONDITION FULFILLED	121
THE SECOND CONDITION FULFILLED	122
THE THIRD CONDITION FULFILED	123
JESUS BECAME OUR HIGH PRIEST	123
PETER'S MESSAGE	125
PETER IN TANNER' HOUSE	127
CORNELIUS'S VISION	128
TANNER	128
PETER'S VISION	131
PETER MEETS CORNELIUS	131
SALVATION TO CORNELIUS	132
CORNELIUS BECOMES MEMBER OF THE CHURCH	134
CHAPTER 24 FOR HIS HOLY NAME SAKE PART I	139
PROPHECY TO THE MOUTAINS OF ISRAEL	139
CHAPTER 25 FOR HIS HOLY NAME PART II	144
THE LORD PUTS HIS SPIRIT WITHIN THEM	145
CHAPTER 26 DRY BONES VISION	150
HIS MARVELOUS WORKS	152
SECTION IV YIELD TO THE CREATOR	156
CHAPTER 27 HE IS THE CREATOR	157
CHAPTER 28 IN THE BEGINNING	162

SECTION V THE SALVATION MESSAGES 166

CHAPTER 29 THE HEAD CORNER STONE 167

CHAPTER 30 "FATHER FORGIVE THEM…" 172

CHAPTER 31 BEHOLD THY SON 176

CHAPTER 32 TODAY SHALT THOU BE WITH ME IN PARADISE 178

CHAPTER 33 ELI, ELI, LAMA SABACHTHANI 183

CHAPTER 34 I THIRST 190

CHAPTER 35 IT IS FINISHED 194

CHAPTER 36 "…FATHER, INTO THY HANDS I COMMEND MY SPIRIT" 198

CHAPTER 37 THE INNER MAN 202

    THE INNER SELF 203

    ON KNEES WHILE PRAYING 203

    ONE FAMILY 204

    FAITH IN THE LORD 204

    BREADTH, LENGTH, DEPTH AND THE HEIGHT 205

    INCREASE IN KNOWLEDGE 206

    PRAISE THE NAME OF THE LORD 207

CHAPTER 38 DO WE CARE? 208

CHAPTER 39 REWARDS FROM RIGHTEOUS JUDGE 210

SECTION I
THE PERSECUTIONS

CHAPTER 1
PERSECUTIONS

PERSECUTION is a "program or campaign to exterminate, drive away, or subjugate people based on their membership in a religious, ethnic, social, or racial group"

PERSECUTION: BIBLICAL DEFINITION

Persecution is an English word translated from Hebrew word (Strong's Number 7291), which is "radaph" pronounced as "raw-daf'" in the Old Testament. The word means to chase, put to flight, follow after, follow on, and/or hunt.

Persecution is an English word translated from Greek word "diogmos", pronounced as "dee-ogue-mos'", (Strong's Number 1375) in the New Testament. The word means to pursue (literally or figuratively); by implication, to persecute:--ensue, follow (after), given to, (suffer) persecute (-ion), press forward. (cf. Greek Strong's Numbers 1169, and1249)

Persecutions exist not only in the New Testament period but they existed in the Old Testament period as well. The greatest persecution found in the Old Testament period was of the killing of prophets by the Jezebel, who was the wicked wife, of King Ahab.

"For it was so, when Jezebel cut off the prophets of the LORD, that Obadiah took an hundred prophets, and hid them by fifty in a cave, and fed them with bread and water" (1 Kings 18:4)

"Was it not told my lord what I did when Jezebel slew the prophets of the LORD, how I hid an hundred men of the LORD'S prophets by fifty in a cave, and fed them with bread and water?" (1 Kings 18:13)

King Manasseh did evil in the sight of the LORD.

"And he made his son pass through the fire, and observed times, and used enchantments, and dealt with familiar spirits and wizards: he wrought much wickedness in the sight of the LORD, to provoke him to anger. And he set a graven image of the grove that he had made in the house, of which the LORD said to David, and to Solomon his son, In this house, and in Jerusalem, which I have chosen out of all tribes of Israel, will I put my name for ever: (2 Kings 21:6-7)

"And also for the innocent blood that he shed: for he filled Jerusalem with innocent blood; which the LORD would not pardon" (2 Kings 24:4)

Lord Jesus Christ said...

"Blessed are they which are persecuted for righteousness' sake: for theirs is the kingdom of heaven" (Matthew 5:10)

When John came neither eating nor drinking people said he has a devil, and when the Son of man came eating and drinking they said He was "gluttonous, and winebibber, a friend of publicans and sinners". Man has tongue and he talks; evil man condemns the righteous either way.

"For John came neither eating nor drinking, and they say, He hath a devil. The Son of man came eating and drinking, and they say, Behold a man gluttonous, and a winebibber, a friend of publicans and sinners. But wisdom is justified of her children" (Matthew 11:18-19)

Jesus never said the lives of the children of God will be pleasant and rid of troubles, trials and persecutions; rather He said that those who would not endure tribulations and persecutions have no root in themselves and, therefore, they are offended. He said blessed are those who suffer persecution for righteousness' sake.

"Yet hath he not root in himself, but dureth for a while: for when tribulation or persecution ariseth because of the word, by and by he is offended" (Matthew 13:21)

A great deal of the nature of persecutions Christians suffer and the blessings they received/or will receive by suffering is found in Mark 10:30 Acts 8:1; Acts 13:50; Romans 8:35 2; Corinthians 12:10 2; Thessalonians 1:4; 2 Timothy 3:11; Matthew 7:1; Luke 9:54-56; Romans 14:4; James 4:11, 12.

Saul, who persecuted the Church and later was known by the name "Paul", said...

"Who shall separate us from the love of Christ? shall tribulation, or distress, or persecution, or famine, or nakedness, or peril, or sword?" (Romans 8:35)

Jesus spoke to Pharisees and Scribes and said to them that their fathers persecuted prophets and they were no better than them. He said that they were getting ready to slay the Messiah and His messengers and to reap the punishment by doing so. Surely as He said their enemies overtook them later as the history reveals. They have upon their heads the curse of killing Abel unto the blood of Zacharias.

"That upon you may come all the righteous blood shed upon the earth, from the blood of righteous Abel unto the blood of

Zacharias son of Barachias, whom ye slew between the temple and the altar" (Matthew 23:35)

Jesus said to His disciples that if the world hated Him and persecuted Him, they will not be reluctant to persecute them as well.

"Remember the word that I said unto you, The servant is not greater than his lord. If they have persecuted me, they will also persecute you; if they have kept my saying, they will keep yours also" (John 15:20)

CHAPTER 2
DISPUTE WITH PHARISEES

"Then again called they the man that was blind, and said unto him, Give God the praise: we know that this man is a sinner" (John 9:24)

Pharisees called Jesus a sinner on the pretext that He healed on the Sabbath day, a man, who was born blind. The man answered Pharisees and said he did not know whether or not Jesus was sinner; but one thing he knew was that he was blind before, and now he has vision to see. They were curious to know the details again.

The man already explained to them very clearly that Jesus spat on the ground, made clay and applied it to his eyes, and because he obeyed His command, and went and washed his eyes in the pool of Siloam, he was healed. Now, when the Pharisees asked him second time, he got annoyed at them and said "I have told you already, and ye did not hear".

How often we listen to someone and yet, we desire the same to be reiterated, because of either unbelief or hesitate to accept the truth. The Pharisees resorted to similar attitude when they asked the man second time as to how he was healed.

The man wondered and asked them if it was because they want to become the disciples of Jesus that they want to hear about the miraculous healing again. When they heard the man speak in contempt they reviled at him saying he was the disciple of Jesus, and they were of Moses.

They ridiculed saying God spoke to them through Moses but as for Jesus, they did not know who He was, and where He came from.

The man had a dig at them saying even though they did not know where Jesus came from, and who He was, yet they marveled at His works. The man, who was born blind and was healed by the Lord, spoke the words of wisdom than did the Pharisees, who were considered to be the wise men of the day.

The man said since the world began, not one incident was heard by anyone; of the kind of healing that Jesus did in him. He boldly testified that if Jesus were not of God, He could have not done anything.

Pharisees were raged in anger and cast him out of their fellowship and synagogue, accusing him that he was born in sins, and asked him how is that he ventured to teach them. They, who were in sins, judged the man that he was born in sins.

"And why beholdest thou the mote that is in thy brother's eye, but considerest not the beam that is in thine own eye?" (Matthew 7:3)

Jesus finding the man asked him if he believed on the Son of God, and the man wondered who the Son of God was. Then Jesus said to him that the man has seen Him, and He, who was talking to him, was the Son of God. Jesus was pointing to Himself.

The man called Jesus as "Lord", which is to say "Master", and said that he believed that Jesus was the Son of God, and worshipped Him.

Jesus said to the man, who was healed of his blindness that blind see and perceive who He was, but those who have sight will be like blind. He judges in order to see that those, who have eyes, may not see, and those, who are blind, may see the truth.

Some of the Pharisees heard the fierce words spoken by Jesus concerning them, and they countered Him, and asked Him if they were blind.

Then, Jesus replied saying, it would have been better if they were blind and not see rather than have eyes and not see the truth. If they said that they were blind their sins would have been forgiven, but because they were boasting that they have eyes their sin remains in them.

"Jesus said unto them, If ye were blind, ye should have no sin: but now ye say, We see; therefore your sin remaineth" (John 9:41)

Apostle Paul writes about Mosaic Law, which the Pharisees were very conversant, and attempted to keep in vain. The Law pointed to the guilt of a person, but it never provided salvation; and surprisingly, Jews, and likewise some in the present generation, try to keep the Law in vain, instead of depending on the grace of our Lord Jesus Christ, and fail miserably in both the cases.

Neither they were able to fulfill the conditions of Mosaic Law, nor do they make attempts to come under the grace of our Lord Jesus Christ. They try to be blind to the truth, and lose sight of the light, and the glorious things that are visible in the light.

"Now we know that what things soever the law saith, it saith to them who are under the law: that every mouth may be stopped, and all the world may become guilty before God. Therefore by the deeds of the law there shall no flesh be justified in his sight: for by the law is the knowledge of sin" (Romans 3:19-20)

The creator is greater than the creation. Worship the creator than the creation. Moses was creation of God and he was a servant of God. Jesus was greater than Moses. Therefore, let us boast in the cleansing power of the blood of Lord Jesus Christ, rather than boasting in Moses.

The LORD gave the Law to the children of Israel though Moses, his servant, and because they failed to keep the Law, Jesus came into the world to die for all sinners that by His grace everyone, who confesses Him as the Lord, and believes in heart that God raised Him from the dead, will become righteous. Salvation belongs to Lord Jesus Christ, and it is by Him alone that one receives everlasting life.

"For this man was counted worthy of more glory than Moses, inasmuch as he who hath builded the house hath more honour than the house. For every house is builded by some man; but he that built all things is God. And Moses verily was faithful in all his house, as a servant, for a testimony of those things which were to be spoken after; But Christ as a son over his own house; whose house are we, if we hold fast the confidence and the rejoicing of the hope firm unto the end" (Hebrews 3:3-6)

CHAPTER 3
THE TRUTH SHALL MAKE YOU FREE

"And ye shall know the truth, and the truth shall make you free" (John 8:32)

The first few verses from John Chapter 8 describe how a woman, who was caught red handedly in the act of prostitution, was brought by Scribes and Pharisees before Jesus, tempting him to determine whether or not she should be punished as per the Law of Moses.

However, Jesus stooped down and wrote something on the ground as if he did not hear them. (cf. John 8:6)

They continued asking him he said to them they may cast stones at her to kill her, but only the man who has never committed any sin in his life may cast first stone at her. None of the accusers threw stones at her and everyone started leaving one by one. Jesus did not condemn the woman and let her go. Scribes and Pharisees still remained there to drag Jesus into debate and catch him on some point and accuse him.

Then Jesus said to Scribes and Pharisees that he was the light of the world and whoever followed him had the light of life and will not walk in darkness. The Pharisees therefore accused him of his birth. When Jesus said to them that He was not alone but he and the Father were one, they did not understand him. They even asked him where his father was.

Jesus told them that the record he bore was true and they knew him not fully well. (John 8:14-15). Jesus was born of the Virgin Mary. Luke 1:35 records… "And the angel answered and said unto her, The Holy Ghost shall come upon thee, and the power of the Highest shall overshadow thee: therefore also that holy thing which shall be born of thee shall be called the Son of God". Jesus is the Son of God.

Jesus said to them that if they knew God they would have known him as well. The argument went on and Pharisees called names and said that he was Samaritan and he had a devil in him. Jesus said that he had no devil in him and they dishonored him but he honored his Father. (John 8:48-50) They did not believe him even though he spoke the Truth.

It can be seen that Jesus was very bold and point blank to give replies to them. Jesus tells them that they need to be freed of their sin. Scribes and Pharisees boasted in themselves that they are the children of Abraham and they were never under bondage that they should be freed from their sin. They did not remember or were ignorant that their forefathers were in bondage of slavery under Pharaoh in Egypt; they did not remember or were ignorant that they were under the bondage of Assyrians and Babylonians.

When they were talking to Jesus, and as they were trying to trap Jesus on some question, they were already under the bondage of Roman Government. Yet, Jesus was making a point that they were under the bondage of sin and they need to be freed of their sin.

Scribes and Pharisees did not realize that Jesus was the Messiah and he was the Son of God. They were claiming that God is their Father and Jesus had to tell them bluntly that their father was devil because they could not recognize the Son of God nor could understand his speech. He said their father, who is the devil,

AMID PERSECUTIONS

was a murderer from the beginning and lived not in the truth because there is no truth in him. (John 8:41-44)

Jesus spoke the truth because He is the Way, He is the Truth and He is the Light. The Pharisees and Scribes lost their patience and were about to harm Jesus. Even as Jesus was speaking these words many believed; yet Scribes and Pharisees went on accusing him and tried to lay hands on him. The time was net yet come, and therefore, no one could do anything to Jesus and he walked away from their midst unharmed.

CHAPTER 4
EVIL BEGETS EVIL

"For the eyes of the Lord are over the righteous, and his ears are open unto their prayers: but the face of the Lord is against them that do evil" 1 Peter 3:12

Never will any evil escape being denounced and evil never begets good. Evil begets evil and the result is destruction of self and others.

Seventh king in Israel was Ahab who was the son of Omri who reigned over Israel in Samaria for twenty two years. Ahab did greater evil than that of any one of his predecessors in the sight of the Lord. As if the evil that he did in the sight of the LORD was not enough he took Jezebel the daughter of Ethbaal king of Zidonians as his wife. Zidonians were the offspring of Sidon, son of Canaan.

"And Canaan begat Sidon his firstborn, and Heth" (Genesis 10:15)

If we trace back to Canaan's lineage he was the son of Ham, who saw his father Noah's nakedness when he was drunk. Ham went and told his brothers, who walked backwards without seeing the nakedness of their father, and covered him. When Noah came to senses from his intoxication he understood what Ham did to him and cursed him saying he will be servant of servants of his brothers (Cf. Genesis 9:19-25).

Ahab married and had very bad ties with the lineage of Cursed Canaan. Ahab's wife Jezebel was wicked woman who brought idol worship into Israel . Not only Ahab and Jezebel worshipped

Baal but they introduced Baal-worship in Israel. Jezebel was the architect of Baal-worship in Israel. Ahab reared up an altar for Baal in the house of Baal and thus Ahab provoked God of Israel to anger more than any one of his predecessors. (cf. 1 Kings 16:29-34)

Ahab was wicked more than any of his predecessors, and he married Jezebel, a wicked woman, of the lineage of Canaan, who was the son of Ham, a cursed son of Noah. Prophet Elijah prophesied that Ahab's family after him will be rooted out completely but only after Ahab's life because he repented in sackcloth.

The result was that Ahab died and was buried with his fathers. (cf. 1 Kings 21:27-29)

Later, at the instructions of Jehu three eunuchs threw Jezebel from out of the window and some of her blood was sprinkled on the wall and on the horses and he trode her under foot and the prophecy of Elijah was fulfilled.

"This is the word of the LORD, which he spake by his servant Elijah the Tishbite, saying, In the portion of Jezreel shall dogs eat the flesh of Jezebel" (cf. 2 Kings 9:33 -36)

"Speak not evil one of another, brethren. He that speaketh evil of his brother, and judgeth his brother, speaketh evil of the law, and judgeth the law: but if thou judge the law, thou art not a doer of the law, but a judge" James 4:11

CHAPTER 5
NABOTH'S VINEYARD

It came to pass that there was a man named Naboth, a Jezrelite, who had a vineyard that was in Jezreel. The vineyard was very close by the palace of Ahab the king of Israel. Once the king spoke to Naboth and said to him sell the vineyard to him for a price or have another vineyard at another place as compensation.

Naboth did not agree to the request because he inherited the vineyard from his forefathers. Ahab was displeased with Naboth and was sad. Ahab's wicked wife Jezebel came to him and asked him as to why he was so sad. Ahab said to Jezebel that he asked Naboth to sell his vineyard to him or have another vineyard as compensation but he refused saying that it was an inheritance from his forefathers.

Jezebel thought it legitimate to grab Naboth's property because her husband is king over the land. She thought it is legitimate to have a citizen's property even when the citizen refuses to sell it. She not only thought it so but adopted very wicked way of grabbing Naboth's vineyard.

Jezebel said to Ahab to get up, eat bread and make merry, because he was the king of Israel and that she would take charge of solving the problem. Jezebel wrote letters in Ahab's name, sealed the letters with Ahab's seal and sent them to the elders and to the nobles in the city living with Naboth. She apparently made Naboth to appear like a criminal although he was exercising what was within his rights. She gathered two false witnesses, who were sons of Belial to witness against Naboth that he blasphemed God and disrespected the king of

Israel. (sons of Belial means the sons of worthless men [Cf. Judges 20:13, 2 Samuel 23:6, 2 Corinthians 6:15).

Jezebel wrote false accusations against Naboth and ordered by the seal of Ahab the king to proclaim fast and set Naboth on high, which is to proclaim that Naboth was a criminal. (It is usual in those days that the criminal is placed in high place to be seen).

After willful and false declaration of Naboth as criminal the elders and the nobles were required to stone him to death. The men of city, the elders and the nobles did just as Jezebel wrote treacherously in the name of her husband and stoned Naboth unto death.

Jezebel went to Ahab and said to him that Naboth is dead and he may go and take possession of his vineyard.

While Ahab was on his way to take possession of the vineyard Elijah came to him with the word of the LORD and said to him:

"... Thus saith the LORD, In the place where dogs licked the blood of Naboth shall dogs lick thy blood, even thine" (1 Kings 21:19 b)

Elijah said of Jezebel saying "...The dogs shall eat Jezebel by the wall of Jezreel" (1 Kings 21:23 b)

The prophecy was fulfilled as written in 1 Kings 21:24-29;1 Kings 22:40; and 2 Kings 9:7-10 and 9:33-36

Persecuting innocent men with false accusations will not go unpunished.

"Then said he unto the disciples, It is impossible but that offences will come: but woe unto him, through whom they come! It were better for him that a millstone were hanged about his neck, and he cast into the sea, than that he should offend one of these little ones" (Luke 17:1-2)

CHAPTER 6
GOD HATES IDOLATRY

"And he reared up an altar for Baal in the house of Baal, which he had built in Samaria. And Ahab made a grove; and Ahab did more to provoke the LORD God of Israel to anger than all the kings of Israel that were before him" (1 Kings 16:32-33)

King Ahab, son of Omri, ruled Samaria in Israel for twenty two years and did evil in the sight of the LORD. During his reign over the "House of Israel", i.e. Northern Kingdom of Israel, the children of Israel worshipped "Baal", which was an idol; a fictitious sun god who they thought was bringing rain for them to cultivate their fields successfully. Ahab married Jezebel, a wicked woman, daughter of Ethbaal, king of Zidoneans, and did evil in the sight of the LORD by building an altar for Baal in the house of Baal in Samaria and provoked the LORD God of Israel by making an image of Ashtoreth, a moon goddess who they thought was a god of fertility (cf. 1 Kings 16:29-34)

Jeroboam the first king of Northern Kingdom of Israel did much harm to the children of Israel by setting up an idol at Beth-haven, the border between Northern kingdom and Southern kingdom; and another idol at Dan, the border on the northern kingdom thus enticing them to worship idols calling them as their god who delivered from the bondage of slavery under Pharaoh. His scheme was to see that the children of Israel, for whom it was mandatory to over to Jerusalem to worship the LORD, do not go over to Jerusalem in the southern region to worship the true and living God (cf. 1 Kings 12:26-27).

The idolatry continued in the "House of Israel" until the LORD scattered them all over the world, beyond any recognition.

None of the nineteen kings who ruled the "House of Israel" did that which was pleasing to the Lord. This perversion increased to great extent in the days of King Ahab and his wicked wife Jezebel.

Elijah the Tishbite who was a true worshipper of the living God and a prophet swore to King Ahab saying "As the LORD God of Israel" lives there will be no dew or rain in those days except for his word. The word of the LORD said to Elijah to go to the brook of "Cheirth", which was before Jordan, and drink from it. Elijah ate food brought to him by ravens in the morning and bread and meat in the evening and drank from the brook just as the LORD provided Manna and quails to the children of Israel in the wilderness water from the Rock but when the brook dried up for want of rain the LORD provided a different means for him to have food at Widow's house (cf. 1 Kings 17:1-7)

Never worship idols; they have ears but cannot hear; they have eyes; but cannot see; they are made of men and often man makes his gods smaller than himself.

"They have mouths, but they speak not: eyes have they, but they see not" (Psalms 115:5)

Trust in the Lord. He is Jehovah-jireh, which means "The Lord will provide". The Psalmist writes:

"I have been young, and now am old; yet have I not seen the righteous forsaken, nor his seed begging bread" (Psalms 37:25)

CHAPTER 7
THE CHALLENGE

Elijah showed up before King Ahab in the third year of famine, as commanded by God, in order that the LORD may send rain upon the earth.

When Ahab saw Elijah he asked Elijah if he was causing trouble in Israel and in response Elijah said to him that it was not he who was causing trouble in Israel, but it was King Ahab who was causing trouble in Israel, by leading the children of Israel away from truth of the LORD, and enticing them to obey Baal, an idol. Elijah said to Ahab that not only his fathers' house have forsaken the commandments of the LORD and worshipped "Baalim"; but he encouraged them to worship idols instead of worshipping the living God.

Inasmuch as Ahab was following Baalim, Elijah threw gauntlets at him for a great show down to see the LORD' s power vis-a-vis the nothingness of idols, and their power, in which Ahab and his family were greatly trusting and relying on. Ahab and his family not only disobeyed the LORD but also made the whole nation to disobey the LORD. They were the cause for children of Israel to forget the commandments of the LORD. In addition his wicked wife had set out herself and slew the LORD's prophets. This enraged the LORD and sent Elijah for a showdown of his strength and power.

Elijah says to Ahab to gather to him all Israel on the Mount Carmel as also the four hundred and fifty prophets of 'Baal', and four hundred groves' prophets who ate at the table of his wife, Jezebel. Ahab agreed and sent word to gather all the children of Israel and the said number of prophets on the Mount Carmel.

When they are all gathered, Elijah questioned them how long they would have two opinions about following the real God and offered them a chance but not a word was heard from them. Then, Elijah said that if they trusted the LORD after seeing the miracle they may follow the LORD or else they may follow Baal. He, then proceeds for a great show down.

Elijah tells them that he was alone standing on behalf of the LORD; presenting himself as the prophet of the LORD, while there are four hundred fifty men standing as prophets of Baal. Elijah challenges and says to the prophets of the Baal to have one bullock and give another to Elijah, and cut their bullock into pieces and lay the pieces on the wood, and put no fire to it, while he would dress the other bullock, cut into pieces and lay the pieces on the wood and put no fire to it.

Elijah said that they should call for their gods and Elijah would call his LORD, and whichever God answers the prayers is the true God and then the children of Israel need to place their trust on the true God. It pleased the children of Israel well.

Elijah told the prophets of Baal to be the first in choosing and dressing one bullock first because they were many and call on the name of their gods, and put no fire under.

"And they took the bullock which was given them, and they dressed it, and called on the name of Baal from morning even until noon, saying, O Baal, hear us. But there was no voice, nor any that answered. And they leaped upon the altar which was made". (1 Kings 18:26 KJV)

The prophets of Baal cried aloud from morning to noon but there was no response from their god. Elijah mocked at the prophets of Baal and said:

"Cry aloud, for he is a god. Either he is musing, or he is relieving himself, or he is on a journey, or perhaps he is asleep and must be awakened." (1 Kings 18:27 ESV)

Prophets of Baal cried aloud several times and cut themselves with knives and lancets until their blood gushed out from their bodies. They cried in vain until evening and their god did not hear them because he has ears but does not hear; and did not answer their prayers nor had any compassion on them who shed blood for him. He did not help them in their dire need of facing challenge to prove their god is true god. Their god neither came to their rescue nor did he save them. All that these worshippers of Baal had at the end of the day was their sweat, tired bodies and the blood that they shed for their god.

Is it not worth pondering that their god could not have compassion on them even though they shed their precious blood for him; just in contrast to our living God, who sent His one and only son, Jesus Christ, who shed His precious blood for our sake, in order that whoever believes in Him shall have eternal life and does not perish? It is our living God, who loved us first, not that we loved him first. He sent his one and only son Jesus Christ for the remission of our sins.

Elijah tells all the people to go near him and he repaired the altar of the LORD that was broken down and took twelve stones according to the number of the tribes of Jacob, whom God loved and renamed him as "Israel".

With the stones he built an altar in the name of the LORD and made around the altar a trench of the size that would contain two measures of seed. He set the wood in order and laid the pieces of the bullock that he cut and ordered the children of Israel, to pour four barrels of water thrice upon the burnt sacrifice, and on the wood in order for the water to run round the altar. In addition, he filled the trench with water.

"And he put the wood in order and cut the bull in pieces and laid it on the wood. And he said, "Fill four jars with water and pour it on the burnt offering and on the wood." And he said, "Do it a second time." And they did it a second time. And he said, "Do it a third time." And they did it a third time. And the water ran around the altar and filled the trench also with water" (1 Kings 18:33-35 ESV)

It is at the time of the offering of the evening sacrifice that Elijah came near and prayed to the LORD, who is the God of Abraham, of Isaac, and of Israel, as follows:

"O LORD, God of Abraham, Isaac, and Israel, let it be known this day that you are God in Israel, and that I am your servant, and that I have done all these things at your word. Answer me, O LORD, answer me, that this people may know that you, O LORD, are God, and that you have turned their hearts back." (1 Kings 18:36-37 ESV)

"Then the fire of the LORD fell and consumed the burnt offering and the wood and the stones and the dust, and licked up the water that was in the trench. And when all the people saw it, they fell on their faces and said, "The LORD, he is God; the LORD, he is God." " (1 Kings 18:38-39 ESV)

This showdown ended really to prove that the LORD was the God of Abraham, Isaac, and Israel, and all the people that saw this miracle fell on their faces and acknowledged that "...The LORD, he is the God; the LORD, he is the God...".

AMID PERSECUTIONS

Elijah did not leave all that there, but he gave instructions to the children of Israel that all the prophets of Baal be taken into custody, making sure that not even one of them escapes. Then they took all the prophets of Baal and brought them down to the brook Kishon where Elijah slaughtered them.

"And Elijah said to them, "Seize the prophets of Baal; let not one of them escape." And they seized them. And Elijah brought them down to the brook Kishon and slaughtered them there" (1 Kings 18:40 ESV)

There was sound of the abundant rain and Elijah said to Ahab to get up, eat and drink. As Ahab went to eat and drink, Elijah went on to the top of Mount Carmel and prayed to God with his face between his knees casting himself down on to the earth. While praying Elijah, asked his servant to go and see if there was rain coming down.

The servant went and came and said, there was no rain, and Elijah did this seven times and lo, there arose a small cloud out the sea like a man's hand. Elijah said to his servant to go to Ahab and say about all these happenings, and prepare for himself a chariot and have a ride to celebrate happiness, and let not the rain stop him. In the meanwhile there came down heavy downpour from heaven, and Ahab rode and went to Jezreel. Elijah had the blessings of having the LORD's hand upon him and, therefore, he also girded his loins up and ran before Ahab to the entrance of Jezreel.

Thus the LORD's name was glorified and everybody trusted in the living God. HE IS THE LIVING GOD. HE IS THE GOD OF GODS (cf. 1 Kings 18:17-46).

CHAPTER 8
ELIJAH CALLS FIRE FROM HEAVEN

"Then Moab rebelled against Israel after the death of Ahab. And Ahaziah fell down through a lattice in his upper chamber that was in Samaria, and was sick: and he sent messengers, and said unto them, Go, enquire of Baalzebub the god of Ekron whether I shall recover of this disease" (2 Kings 1:1-2)

After the death of King Ahab his son Ahazia took over reigns of Northern Kingdom of Israel which was at its lowest ebb in their spiritual life. Idolatry started during the period of Jeroboam the first king of Northern Kingdom and during the period of Ahab his wicked wife Jezebel introduced "Baal" worship. The children of Israel have become so addicted to worshipping "Baal" that when Elijah pleaded them to return to God and accept Him as LORD, they did not speak a word. Subsequently he challenged them and proved that the God Abraham, of Isaac and of Israel was the true God.

Now when Ahazia became King he did evil in the sight of the LORD just as his father did. One day he fell through lattice in his upper chamber in Samaria and lay sick. In order to know whether he would be healed or not he sent his messengers with instructions to go and inquire "Baal-zeebub" the god of "Ekron". Ekron was an ancient city of Philistines. Joshua did not subdue it but it was allotted to him in the division of the land initially to Judah and later on to Dan (cf. Joshua 13:3; Joshua 15:11, 45-46; 19:43. The name of the city Ekron figures in the narration when Philistines feared presence of the Ark of the Covenant in their land and the proposed to send it back to Israel (Cf. 1Sa 5:10; 6:16-17)

Hebrew Word Strong's# 1176 "Ba`al Z@buwb" is transliterated as "bah'-al zeb-oob'", originated from Strong's# 1168 and 2070 and its definition is "Baal of (the) Fly; Baal-Zebub, a special deity of the Ekronites:--"Baal-zebub" and is also called the "Baal of the Flies" or "lord of the flies".

Lord Jesus Christ referred to "Baal-zebub" mentioned in the Old Testament as "Beelzebul", which in Greek was called "Beelzebul" (Greek Strong's# 954 transliterated as "beh-el-zeb-ool'" of Chaldee origin (by parody on H1176) which "dung-god"; Beelzebul, a name of Satan, Beelzebub.

"But when the Pharisees heard it, they said, This fellow doth not cast out devils, but by Beelzebub the prince of the devils. And Jesus knew their thoughts, and said unto them, Every kingdom divided against itself is brought to desolation; and every city or house divided against itself shall not stand: And if Satan cast out Satan, he is divided against himself; how shall then his kingdom stand? And if I by Beelzebub cast out devils, by whom do your children cast them out? therefore they shall be your judges. But if I cast out devils by the Spirit of God, then the kingdom of God is come unto you" (Matthew 12:24-28)

The LORD was highly displeased with Ahazia who sent messengers to Ekron to inquire from the Baal-zebub "Lord of the Flies", whom he was worshipping to know if he would be healed or not. The LORD therefore, sent Elijah the Tishbite to question him if there was no God in Israel that Ahazia should send messengers to inquire from someone who is lord over flies.

It is so pathetic that man worships creation rather than Creator. Flies are indeed created marvelously by God but they are creation and not creator. They are worth only to be seen as creation and do not deserve any worship. Satan has closed the understanding of people who condescend to worshipping flies, snakes, trees, and rocks.

Bible condemns worshiping creation rather than creator. Messengers of Ahazia returned to the king and the king asked him as to why they returned. They said to him that they saw a man who ordered them to return to say to the king that to question him if there was no God in Israel that he should send them to inquire from Baal-zebub, the god of Ekron if he would be healed or not.

The Messengers also said that the man said to them that the king will be bed-ridden until his death. Ahazia was curious to know who that man was, and how he looked like. They answered and said to him that he "wore a garment of hair, with a belt of leather about his waist." Ahazia recognized him and said, "It is Elijah the Tishbite."

Ahazia, in his authority as King, sent a captain over fifty men with his fifty men to bring Elijah to him. The captain went up to Elijah who was sitting on the top of a hill and said to him "O man of God, the king says, 'Come down.'"

The captain in his authority and power, vested in him by the king, was ordering Elijah the Tishbite who was sent by the Almighty God the King of kings. It was derogatory to order the "man of God" to come down from the place where he was sitting and stand before the king of earthly kingdom.

Elijah answered the captain of fifty saying "If I am a man of God, let fire come down from heaven and consume you and your fifty." Elijah called fire from heaven and the fire came down from heaven and consumed the captain and his fifty men.

AMID PERSECUTIONS

When a similar situation occurred in the New Testament period, when Lord Jesus Christ was not received by Samaritans, his disciples James and John inquired of Lord Jesus Christ if they should call for fire from heaven and consume them just as Elijah did; but Lord Jesus prevented such drastic action. He was so compassionate towards those who did not receive Him and rebuked His disciples.

"But he turned, and rebuked them, and said, Ye know not what manner of spirit ye are of. For the Son of man is not come to destroy men's lives, but to save them. And they went to another village" (cf. Luke 9:51-56)

Lord Jesus came into this world in the form of a servant and in the likeness of man and died on the cross taking our sin upon Him even though He was sinless. He was buried and was raised by God. Paul writes that whoever confesses Jesus as Lord and believes in heart that God raised Him from the dead will be saved. Lord Jesus promised that whoever believes in Him shall not perish but have everlasting life. (cf. Romans 10:9 and John 3:16)

Ahazia sent to Elijah another captain of fifty men with his fifty men to bring him, and the captain added his power to the king's power, and said to the man of God, "O man of God, this is the king's order, 'Come down quickly!'" but Elijah answered saying "'If I am a man of God, let fire come down from heaven and consume you and your fifty' Then the fire of God came down from heaven and consumed him and his fifty".

As if this was not enough for Ahazia he sent a third captain of fifty men with his fifty men to bring Elijah to his presence. This time the third captain fell on his knees and begged Elijah saying, "O man of God, please let my life, and the life of these fifty servants of yours, be precious in your sight. Behold, fire came down from heaven and consumed the two former captains of fifty men with their fifties, but now let my life be precious in your sight."

Before Elijah called fire from heaven this time the angel of the LORD said to him to go with the third captain fearlessly and, therefore, he went with him and said to the king "Thus says the LORD, 'Because you have sent messengers to inquire of Baal-zebub, the god of Ekron—is it because there is no God in Israel to inquire of his word?—therefore you shall not come down from the bed to which you have gone up, but you shall surely die.'"

According to the word of the LORD by the mouth of Elijah, Ahazia the king died. (cf. 2 Kings 1-18)

CHAPTER 9
GOD SPOKE IN SMALL STILL VOICE

"And after the earthquake a fire; [but] the LORD [was] not in the fire: and after the fire a still small voice" 1 Kings 19:12

During the journey of Israelites in the wilderness God spoke to Moses several times. One such incidence is found in Exodus 19:16-19. There were thunders and lightening and a thick cloud upon the Mount Sinai The trumpet sound was exceedingly loud and the people trembled. While the people waited near the Mount Sinai God descended upon it in fire and smoke ascended as the smoke from a furnace. Mount Sinai was on a smoke and God responded to Moses in a voice.

In 1 Kings 18:20-40 there is a dramatic presentation of how Elijah proved that Jehovah is the real God, the God of heaven and earth, the God who created heavens, earth, seas and all that is therein. Baal and four hundred and fifty prophets of Baal were humiliated and Elijah killed them all. The idol remained an idol speechless. God showed up on Mount Carmel in the form of fire and consumed the burnt sacrifice offered by Elijah.

Elijah was afraid of the threatening made by Jezebel, wife of wicked king, Ahab. She threatened to kill Elijah, and somehow Elijah's fear exceeded the success he had seen earlier. He went and hid in a cave where an angel of the Lord appeared to him and asked him to be courageous, rise and eat. Elijah obeyed and rose and ate for forty days and forty nights on the mount.

The LORD said to Elijah to stand upon the mount and Elijah did as the LORD said to him. God passed by and behold there was great and strong wind rent the mountains and broke the rocks but He was not there. After this an earthquake took place and after earthquake a fire, but the LORD was not in the fire, but after the fire there God came to Elijah in a small still voice and spoke to him.

The word of the LORD came to Elijah and asked him "What doest thou here, Elijah?" Prophet Elijah answered the LORD God of hosts that he was very jealous for the LORD and while the children of Israel forsook the covenant, he was all alone left to stand for the LORD and his life is being sought after. God said to Elijah that there were He reserved seven thousand in Israel who did not bow their knees to Baal.

"Yet I have left [me] seven thousand in Israel, all the knees which have not bowed unto Baal, and every mouth which hath not kissed him" 1 Kings 19:18

In the following references we see that God spoke in fire, thunder, whirlwind besides speaking in still small voice.

Job 37:2 "Hear attentively the noise of his voice, and the sound [that] goeth out of his mouth"

Job 38:1 "Then the LORD answered Job out of the whirlwind, and said" Psalm 104:7 "At thy rebuke they fled; at the voice of thy thunder they hasted away.

Zechariah 4:6 Then he answered and spake unto me, saying, This [is] the word of the LORD unto Zerubbabel, saying, Not by might, nor by power, but by my spirit, saith the LORD of hosts"

John 12:29 "The people therefore, that stood by, and heard [it], said that it thundered: others said, An angel spake to him"

Revelation 4:5 "And out of the throne proceeded lightnings and thunderings and voices: and [there were] seven lamps of fire burning before the throne, which are the seven Spirits of God"

Thus we see that God spoke to man in different ways in different periods and the writer of Hebrews rightly said:

"God, who at sundry times and in divers manners spake in time past unto the fathers by the prophets, Hath in these last days spoken unto us by [his] Son, whom he hath appointed heir of all things, by whom also he made the worlds" Hebrews 1:1-2

CHAPTER 10
JEZEBEL'S DEATH

It was time for Jehu to showdown his strength. He rode his chariot furiously to the city of Jezreel where king Jehoram (9th King of Israel) and Ahaziah (6th King of Judah) were rendezvous at Joram's palace. Jeroboam was the first king of the Northern Kingdom of Israel, King Ahab was the seventh King and Jehu was the tenth King.

One soldier went down on horseback at the behest of Joram and questioned Jehu if he was coming in peace. Jehu ridiculed him and pushed the soldier behind him and said to him to follow. At the report of watchman Joram sent another soldier to Jehu, and he questioned Jehu if he was coming in peace. Jehu ridiculed and pushed the second soldier also behind him and said to him to follow.

Then, Joram and Ahazia decided to throw the gauntlets and went each on his chariot to fight against Jehu. They met Jehu in the field of Naboth of Jezreel, where Jezebel the wicked queen, wife of wicked king Ahab, killed Naboth by trickery. Joram inquired Jehu if he was coming in peace and Jehu reminded him of his Grandmother Jezebel's whoredoms and her witchcrafts which were plenty in number to reckon.

Joram and Ahazia sensed treachery and tried to flee from Jehu, but he killed both the kings, one after another, and gave testimony that God laid on his heart a burden to avenge the blood of Naboth and his children. Joram's dead body was thrown in the field of Naboth. Ahaziah, who was fleeing with injuries, died at Megiddo. Ahaziah's servants carried his dead body to Jerusalem where they laid his body to rest with his fathers in the city of David.

Jehu returned to Jezreel and was encountered by Jezebel the wicked wife of Ahab. Jehu shouted inquiring if there was anyone on his side and there were two or three eunuchs looked out to him from the window. Jehu said to them to throw Jezebel down from the window. While Jezebel fell she hit the wall and died. Her blood was sprinkled on the wall. Jehu trod Jezebel under his feet.

Jehu came in to the house and while eating said to them to go and bury Jezebel. Jehu thought of paying her last respects because she was not only queen but was also a daughter of king Ethbaal. They went to the place where Jezebel died; but they did not see her dead body. They came to Jehu and said to him that they found no more of her than her skull, feet and the palms. Then Jehu recollected before them the prophecy of Elijah the Tishbite who said "In the portion of Jezreel shall dogs eat the flesh of Jezebel: And the carcase of Jezebel shall be as dung upon the face of the field in the portion of Jezreel; so that they shall not say, This is Jezebel" (Ref. 2 Kings 9:37)

"And of Jezebel also spake the LORD, saying, The dogs shall eat Jezebel by the wall of Jezreel" (1 Kings 21:23)

CHAPTER 11
PERSECUTIONS IN THE NEW TESTAMENT

It is seen from the church history that during Peter's time there were five major persecutions and thereafter, during Paul's time there were few more. Apostle Paul, who before his conversion persecuted the church, and he was then known by the name Saul. After his conversion, Paul fervently worked for the Lord, and while working for the growth of the church, suffered enormous persecution. It is interesting to see that in the midst of these persecutions the church grew so strong that Christianity is the largest among all the religions of the world today. The following are the five major persecutions seen in the early days of Church history.

1. First persecution is described in Acts 4: 1-31
2. Second persecution is described in Acts 5:17-6:7
3. Third persecution is described in Acts 6:8-60
4. Fourth persecution is described in Acts 8:1-11:30
5. Fifth persecution is described in Acts 12:1-17

First persecution: Peter and John were questioned for healing the lame man. The authorities prohibited them from speaking about Jesus; however Peter and John defiantly pursued in preaching Jesus and the Gospel of Jesus Christ.

Second Persecution: Peter and John were arrested and put in prison but the angel of the Lord delivered them from the prison.

Third Persecution: Stephen was questioned. He tells them the whole history of Israel; but the authorities stoned him to death.

While he was breathing his last he prayed to God to forgive his persecutors.

Fourth Persecution: Saul persecuted the Church and was encountered by Lord Jesus. Saul turned to the Lord and he became a great preacher of Jesus.

Fifth Persecution: Peter was arrested and put in Jail but God let him out of prison miraculously.

Thereafter there are numerous occasions when Paul was persecuted.

CHAPTER 12
THE FIRST PERSECUTION

PETER AND JOHN THREATENED

In the early days when the Church came into existence, Apostle Peter and Apostle John preached boldly and healed a lame man who was forty years old.

"And a certain man lame from his mother's womb was carried, whom they laid daily at the gate of the temple which is called Beautiful, to ask alms of them that entered into the temple" (Acts 3:2)

They healed the lame in the name of Lord Jesus Christ.

"Then Peter said, Silver and gold have I none; but such as I have give I thee: In the name of Jesus Christ of Nazareth rise up and walk" (Acts 3:6) The rulers, and elders persecuted Peter and John for preaching the word of God

"And it came to pass on the morrow, that their rulers, and elders, and scribes, And Annas the high priest, and Caiaphas, and John, and Alexander, and as many as were of the kindred of the high priest, were gathered together at Jerusalem. And when they had set them in the midst, they asked, By what power, or by what name, have ye done this? Then Peter, filled with the Holy Ghost, said unto them, Ye rulers of the people, and elders of Israel, If we this day be examined of the good deed done to the impotent man, by what means he is made whole; Be it known unto you all, and to all the people of Israel, that by the name of Jesus Christ of Nazareth, whom ye crucified, whom

God raised from the dead, even by him doth this man stand here before you whole" (Acts 4:5-10)

Peter and John witnessed boldly and refused to pay heed to the orders of rulers, who threatened them with dire consequences.

"If we this day be examined of the good deed done to the impotent man, by what means he is made whole; Be it known unto you all, and to all the people of Israel, that by the name of Jesus Christ of Nazareth, whom ye crucified, whom God raised from the dead, even by him doth this man stand here before you whole. This is the stone which was set at nought of you builders, which is become the head of the corner. Neither is there salvation in any other: for there is none other name under heaven given among men, whereby we must be saved" (Acts 4:9-12)

"But Peter and John answered and said unto them, Whether it be right in the sight of God to hearken unto you more than unto God, judge ye. For we cannot but speak the things which we have seen and heard. So when they had further threatened them, they let them go, finding nothing how they might punish them, because of the people: for all men glorified God for that which was done". (Acts 4:19-21)

The Church and the preachers were persecuted in different ways, but in none of the cases the opponents of Church were successful. Not even Saul, who persecuted the Church was successful and Jesus Himself intervened and said to Saul

"And he said, Who art thou, Lord? And the Lord said, I am Jesus whom thou persecutest: it is hard for thee to kick against the pricks" (Acts 9:5)

Saul became a great Preacher and was known by the name "Paul". The Church always grew amid Persecutions.

"Then they that gladly received his word were baptized: and the same day there were added unto them about three thousand souls" (Acts 2:41)

"Howbeit many of them which heard the word believed; and the number of the men was about five thousand" (Acts 4:4)

As records indicate there are TWO BILLION Christians in the world today.

(Source: https://www.cia.gov/library/publications/the-world-factbook/fields/2122.html#xx)

"Being grieved that they taught the people, and preached through Jesus the resurrection from the dead. And they laid hands on them, and put them in hold unto the next day: for it was now eventide. Howbeit many of them which heard the word believed; and the number of the men was about five thousand" (Acts 4:2-4)

The boldness of Peter and John waxed strong as they spoke unto people the Gospel of Jesus Christ. The Priests, the captain of the temple, and Sadducees were grieved when they preached through Jesus Christ the resurrection from the dead. They were all greatly perturbed to hear about resurrection and life after death. Sadducees did not believe that life exists after death.

One great comfort Christians, who are saved by the blood of Jesus Christ, have is that the soul of believer never perishes but lives eternally with Lord. In Lord Jesus Christ is salvation and resurrection and everlasting life. We will see Him face to face and live with Him forever and ever.

Apostle Paul explains elaborately in 1 Corinthians 15:12-58 about resurrection. When our corruptible bodies put on incorruption, and our mortality turns into immortality, then we will say "Death is swallowed up in victory. O death, where is thy sting? O grave, where is thy victory? The sting of death is sin; and the strength of sin is the law" (cf. Isaiah 25:8; Hebrew 11:29)

The preaching of this fact was not pleasing to the jealous authorities, who were gradually losing their importance in public life, as more and more people believed in the Gospel of Jesus Christ. They laid hands on Peter and John and held them captive until the next day. Their efforts to inhibit the preaching of the Gospel did not prevail over the tremendous wave of the power of the message of Christ and resurrection was taught to the people. The result was seen when the number of the men, who believed in Lord Jesus were about five thousand.

The rulers, the elders, scribes, Annas the high priest, and Caiphas, John, Alexander and the entire clan of the high priest gathered the next day at Jerusalem. They set Peter and John in their midst and questioned them by what power or by what name they healed the lame man, who was impotent in his legs from birth.

When Jesus was on this earth he taught not to fear those who have power over the body, but fear the One, who is able to destroy both soul and body in hell. God's grace is enough to suffer persecution and the scripture says blessed are those who are persecuted.

"Blessed are they which are persecuted for righteousness' sake: for theirs is the kingdom of heaven" (Matthew 5:10)

All that a man, who persecutes, can do is to destroy the fleshly body of the persecuted ones and never the inner man of the believer. Although we do not have the details as to whether or not the persecuted ones suffer pain during persecution, yet one thing is sure that God will be with the one who suffers it to redeem from it. Who knows, God can kill the pain; nonetheless, even if one suffers pain and tastes death, it would be for the Lord's glory. Did not the Lord suffer and taste the death when He was on the cross? And if so, then, as the Lord said, "Blessed are they which are persecuted for righteousness' sake: for theirs is the kingdom of heaven" (Matthew 5:10)

The Lord gave a clear consolation and said, fear the one who is able to destroy soul and body. No man can destroy a believer's soul.

"And fear not them which kill the body, but are not able to kill the soul: but rather fear him which is able to destroy both soul and body in hell" (Matthew 10:28)

Peter, who was filled with Holy Spirit witnessed to them boldly...

"...Ye rulers of the people, and elders of Israel, If we this day be examined of the good deed done to the impotent man, by what means he is made whole; Be it known unto you all, and to all the people of Israel, that by the name of Jesus Christ of Nazareth, whom ye crucified, whom God raised from the dead, even by him doth this man stand here before you whole. (Acts 4:8-10)

HEALING OF LAME MAN

In the early days when the Church came into existence, Apostle Peter and Apostle John preached boldly and healed a lame man who was forty years old.

"And a certain man lame from his mother's womb was carried, whom they laid daily at the gate of the temple which is called Beautiful, to ask alms of them that entered into the temple" (Acts 3:2)

They healed the lame in the name of Lord Jesus Christ.

"Then Peter said, Silver and gold have I none; but such as I have give I thee: In the name of Jesus Christ of Nazareth rise up and walk" (Acts 3:6)

AMID PERSECUTIONS

The rulers, and elders persecuted Peter and John for preaching the word of God

"And it came to pass on the morrow, that their rulers, and elders, and scribes, And Annas the high priest, and Caiaphas, and John, and Alexander, and as many as were of the kindred of the high priest, were gathered together at Jerusalem. And when they had set them in the midst, they asked, By what power, or by what name, have ye done this? Then Peter, filled with the Holy Ghost, said unto them, Ye rulers of the people, and elders of Israel, If we this day be examined of the good deed done to the impotent man, by what means he is made whole; Be it known unto you all, and to all the people of Israel, that by the name of Jesus Christ of Nazareth, whom ye crucified, whom God raised from the dead, even by him doth this man stand here before you whole" (Acts 4:5-10)

However, Peter and John witnessed boldly and refused to pay heed to the orders rulers, who threatened with dire consequences.

"If we this day be examined of the good deed done to the impotent man, by what means he is made whole; Be it known unto you all, and to all the people of Israel, that by the name of Jesus Christ of Nazareth, whom ye crucified, whom God raised from the dead, even by him doth this man stand here before you whole. This is the stone which was set at nought of you builders, which is become the head of the corner. Neither is there salvation in any other: for there is none other name under heaven given among men, whereby we must be saved" (Acts 4:9-12)

"But Peter and John answered and said unto them, Whether it be right in the sight of God to hearken unto you more than unto

God, judge ye. For we cannot but speak the things which we have seen and heard. So when they had further threatened them, they let them go, finding nothing how they might punish them, because of the people: for all men glorified God for that which was done". (Acts 4:19-21)

The Church and the preachers were persecuted in different ways, but in none of the cases the opponents of Church were successful. Not even Saul, who persecuted the Church was successful and Jesus Himself intervened and said to Saul

"And he said, Who art thou, Lord? And the Lord said, I am Jesus whom thou persecutest: it is hard for thee to kick against the pricks" (Acts 9:5)

Saul became a great Preacher and was known by the name "Paul". The Church always grew amid Persecutions.

"Then they that gladly received his word were baptized: and the same day there were added unto them about three thousand souls" (Acts 2:41)

"Howbeit many of them which heard the word believed; and the number of the men was about five thousand" (Acts 4:4)

As records indicate there are TWO BILLION Christians in the world today.

(Source: https://www.cia.gov/library/publications/the-world-factbook/fields/2122.html#xx)

IN THE NAME OF JESUS

It all started when Peter and John were on their way to the Temple at the ninth hour for prayer, when they saw a man of 40 years of age, lame in his legs, lying at the gate called "Beautiful" of the temple. He was lame from the time when he was in his mother's womb. Those who helped him laid him daily at the gate of the temple, in order that he may make his life by ask and receive alms at that gate.

Peter and John were entering the temple, when the lame man asked alms just as he was asking anyone else. They felt compassion on him and Peter said to him that they had neither silver nor gold to give to him but said he would give what he had. Peter said to the lame man "...In the name of Jesus Christ of Nazareth rise up and walk" (Acts 3:6)

Peter took him by the right hand, and lifted him up. The lame man received strength in his ankle and stood up immediately leaping up and he walked. He did not stop there, but entered into the temple walking and leaping and praising God.

The people, who saw him walk, also praised God as the lame man did. They saw him daily at the "Beautiful" gate of the temple asking alms from the visitors and when they saw him walk and leap with joy they marveled. As they stood in amazement Peter spoke elaborately praising God instead of taking credit for himself. He knew that he was only an instrument in the hands of God, and being an instrument could not heal or do any miracle by himself, and therefore, gave acknowledged the works of the Lord Jesus Christ.

Peter questioned the people as to why they were marveling or why they looked at him and John so earnestly as if they healed the lame by their power or holiness. They acknowledged that the God of Abraham, and of Isaac, and of Jacob and the God of their fathers, who glorified His Son Jesus, whom the men of

AMID PERSECUTIONS

Israel delivered up and denied in the presence of Pontius Pilate, even as Pilate was determined to let go Jesus.

Pilate declared Jesus as "just" and yet delivered Him to be crucified even though Jesus did nothing that deserved death. People preferred a murderer, whose name was Barabbas, to be released instead of Jesus. Peter and John were witnesses to the death of innocent Lord Jesus, the Prince of life, but God raised Him from the dead. Jesus was buried in the grave and grave could not hold him up, nor was His body corrupted.

In that powerful name of Lord Jesus of Nazareth through faith was the lame man healed. The lame man became, whom the people saw daily at the "Beautiful" gate of the temple strong, and rightly as the Lord Jesus deserved worship and praise, Peter gave credit to the Lord and said that the name of Jesus of Nazareth and in His name through faith was the lame man, whom they saw, was made strong. He admonished that they did it in their ignorance and, therefore, they should repent and be converted that their sins may be blotted out (cf. Acts 3:12-20)

Similar offer is available even today that if we confess by mouth our sins to the Lord and accept Him as the Lord, and believe in heart that God raised Him from the dead, we receive salvation and everlasting life to be with the Lord forever and ever. Every sin, except that of blasphemy of Holy Spirit is forgivable by Lord Jesus Christ.

"That if thou shalt confess with thy mouth the Lord Jesus, and shalt believe in thine heart that God hath raised him from the dead, thou shalt be saved" (Romans 10:9)

"Neither is there salvation in any other: for there is none other name under heaven given among men, whereby we must be saved" (Acts 4:12)

MIRACLES

"Neither is there salvation in any other: for there is none other name under heaven given among men, whereby we must be saved" (Acts 4:12)

Bible Encyclopedia and Webster's dictionary define "miracle" as "an event or effect contrary to the established constitution and course of things, or a deviation from the known laws of nature; a supernatural event. Miracles can be wrought only by Almighty power, as when Christ healed lepers, saying, "I will, be thou clean," or calmed the tempest, "Peace, be still."

There are at least 123 miracles recorded in the Bible (Old Testament and New Testament (Ref: http://www.christiananswers.net/dictionary/miracle.html). However, according to Apostle John there are many other things which Jesus did that are not recorded.

Miracles are not confined to healing diseases but they are seen happening in many ways. They were seen in Old Testament period as also in New Testament period. Some examples of miracles that are not healing are:

Old Testament:

- Balaam's Donkey speaks to Balaam (Numbers 22:21-35);
- Samson's strength (Judges Ch. 14-16);

- David obeys the Lord and smites the Philistines when "the sound of a going in the tops of the mulberry trees" was heard (2 Samuel 5:23-25) etc.

New Testament:

- Water turned to wine (John 2:1-11);

- Wise men saw in the east the star that led them to Bethlehem where Jesus was born (Matthew 2: 9);

- Tribute money was found in the mouth of the fish (Matthew 17:24-27) etc.

"And there are also many other things which Jesus did, the which, if they should be written every one, I suppose that even the world itself could not contain the books that should be written. Amen" (John 21:25)

In the early days when the disciples of Jesus Christ and Apostle Paul preached the Gospel they did miracles, in the name of Jesus of Nazareth, and they saw healing taking place instantly. These miracles helped people to seek God more earnestly and thus the Church grew fast and great. Miracles happen only at the discretion of the Lord, and in His time, and according to His will. No one can invoke the power of God to instantly heal a person. Miracles, similar to the ones that happened during the period of Jesus and/or Apostles, are not happening these days. "Faith-healing" miracles that we see now-a-days have proven more as hoax rather than real.

It should *not* be misconstrued that God's wisdom or ability is being questioned here. God surely delivers His children from troubles, trials, and accidents, and untoward incidents, and infections. God also surely shows the ways, provides means, help and resources to get cured of any disease. However, it is all up to God to answer prayer in accordance with His will and pleasure. No one can invoke God's power at one's discretion. Apostle Paul prayed three times for removal of the thing that was bothering him but God said His grace was enough.

"For this thing I besought the Lord thrice, that it might depart from me. And he said unto me, My grace is sufficient for thee: for my strength is made perfect in weakness. Most gladly therefore will I rather glory in my infirmities, that the power of Christ may rest upon me" (2 Corinthians 12:8-9)

Apostle Paul gave advise to Timothy to take medicine for healing.

"Drink no longer water, but use a little wine for thy stomach's sake and thine often infirmities" (1 Timothy 5:23)

It is my personal testimony that my kidneys failed in 1996, and after having had 84 dialyses, I had kidney transplantation in February 1997. Since then, it is purely by the grace of God that I am living. God has been providing me sources, finance and medicines until this day. Praise the Lord.

When Jesus performed miracles He did not adopt one single method of healing. There were many who were healed instantly, and there was also a blind man, who was commanded to go and wash in the pool of Siloam the clay that the Lord made by spitting on the ground, and anointing the eyes of the blind man (John 9:7-11). This is the method that we see now and God helping His children by providing means and sources that would heal a person.

God helps heal a disease in a person with or without the aid of medication. As Jesus said there would come many in His name and do wonders, there are already who do miracles in His name, but in reality these miracles are like the ones that the magicians did during Moses' time. The staff of Moses which turned into serpent, when Aaron threw it on the ground, swallowed up the serpents of the magicians.

"For they cast down every man his rod, and they became serpents: but Aaron's rod swallowed up their rods" (Exodus 7:12)

MIRACLES DO HAPPEN

"He shall cover thee with his feathers, and under his wings shalt thou trust: his truth shall be thy shield and buckler" (Psalms 91:4)

It may appear trivial to those who do not believe in God's miraculous help in times of our trouble, but it was a true happening in my life last year (2014), on a winter night, when I was driving at about 11.00 PM when my car went over a construction zone and had a flat tire.

In that inclement weather, on that night, I, with my failing health, could hardly get out of my car to change the tire. I pulled-over car to the shoulder and prayed to God seeking help. Surprisingly, there came a car and stopped by my car. The driver, who was a dark skinned young man, probably in his forties, perhaps of the character of Good Samaritan, asked me if I needed some help. I gladly accepted his help and told him that my car had flat tire. Soon, the man in his car made U-turn and focused his car-headlights on to my car and stepped out of his car. I took out the spare tire from the trunk of my car and handed it over to him.

While he was fixing the tire a Government official's car came by and stopped near my car. It was very unusual that that the man, in his car, got out and came walking to me and asked me if everything was alright. I told him that my car had flat tire, and someone is helping me. The officer walked to the man and asked him if he was helping me. He said "yes, sir". Then, the officer went back to his car and watched us for some time and drove away from the scene. I just could not spot the officer's car until it came very near to me, and similarly I could not spot the car as he drove away from us. It just vanished in no time!

The man, who was helping me, fixed the tire and was about to go. I said to him I have only credit cards and $4.00 in cash. He said nothing, but kept looking at me as if he was telling me that he did not ask anything in return for his help. However, I forced him to accept all that had in cash on that night and thanked him for the help. He did not refuse to oblige me and accepted money and also accepted my thanks and drove away his car bidding me good-bye. Although my offering was no significance, an instant thought came to my mind as if I was offering him something as Abraham offered his tithe to Melchizedek.

"And Melchizedek king of Salem brought forth bread and wine: and he was the priest of the most high God. And he blessed him, and said, Blessed be Abram of the most high God, possessor of heaven and earth: And blessed be the most high God, which hath delivered thine enemies into thy hand. And he gave him tithes of all" (Genesis 14:18-20)

I thanked God so much that, I could not for a moment believe that such help could come from God. I paused and thought for some time who those two men were, who helped me. In all possibility I believe they were angels; I do not know. It was, surely a memorable incident. Thank God.

The miracles by themselves are neither a means of preaching the Gospel nor do they save a person from eternal damnation. At the outset the person upon whom the miracle is performed should have confessed Jesus as the Lord and thereafter believed in heart that God raised Jesus from the dead on the third day.

However, that pops up another question as to whether or not healing that takes place in the patients of other religions, when they believe in divine power and His provision of medications, is believable or not. Again, it is to be reiterated here that miracles, and miraculous healing are not the means of salvation, but they are a way to trust God in a dearest way.

The knowledge of the Truth is to be sought to know the living God and His provision for salvation. Peter says there is no salvation in any other except in Jesus Christ and we believe it is the Truth. No one can earn salvation by his/her righteous works for the simple reason that man can never become perfect and righteous.

"We have all become like one who is unclean, and all our righteous deeds are like a polluted garment. We all fade like a leaf, and our iniquities, like the wind, take us away" (Isaiah 64:6 ESV)

"Come now, and let us reason together, saith the LORD: though your sins be as scarlet, they shall be as white as snow; though they be red like crimson, they shall be as wool" (Isaiah 1:18)

The authorities and rulers perceived as Peter and John boldly proclaimed the Gospel of Jesus Christ that they were uneducated and common men, and yet because they were with Jesus they had divine knowledge. They saw the man, who was lam and was healed and the man was live standing beside them, and, therefore, they could not say anything to Peter and John in opposition. They conferred among themselves as to how they could force them not to preach the Gospel of Jesus Christ. They could not. The lame man and his healing were so evident to the entire inhabitants of Jerusalem that they could not deny the notable miracle that was performed upon him.

The rulers adopted a tricky way of persecution by charging them not to speak or teach at all in the name of Jesus anymore. However, the courage of Peter and John waxed great and they argued with the rulers asking them, "Whether it is right in the sight of God to listen to you rather than to God, you must judge, for we cannot but speak of what we have seen and heard."

Then the rulers and the authorities saw no way to punish them and, therefore, let them go. They were afraid of people, who praised God for the miracle that had happened in the life of the lame man, who was forty years of age (cf. Acts 4:13-22)

It is the courage of servants of God, and the people who can talk to the authorities, that brings results.

PRAISE AND WORSHIP

"And when they heard it, they lifted their voices together to God and said, "Sovereign Lord, who made the heaven and the earth and the sea and everything in them" (Acts 4:24 ESV)

Peter and John were let go by the chief priests and elders who in vain tried to prevent them from preaching the Gospel of Jesus Christ. People knew that the miracle performed by them was from God. Peter himself had acknowledged that John and he were only the instruments in the hands of God and it was God who healed the lame man.

Peter and John went to their friends' house, after being let go by the authorities, and told them all that had happened to them as a consequence of the healing of the lame man by the hand of God through them. When they heard the news they lifted their voices and praised God, acknowledging that the Lord was Sovereign, and it is He who made the heaven and the earth and everything in them, and also the sea and everything in it.

The LORD spoke by the mouth of David many years ago and questioned as to why the kings of the earth do set themselves in rage against the LORD and imagine in vain things against Him and His anointed Son, Lord Jesus Christ, saying "Let us burst their bonds apart and cast away their cords from us." The LORD who sits on the throne laughs at them in derision and says to Jesus Christ that He is the begotten Son of God.

The Father said to the Son that He gave the nations as heritage to the Son, and the ends of the earth as His possession. Lord Jesus Christ, who is the Son of God, will "break them with a rod of iron and dash them in pieces like potter's vessel".

KISS THE SON

"Kiss the Son, lest he be angry, and ye perish from the way, when his wrath is kindled but a little. Blessed are all they that put their trust in him". (Psalms 2:12)

Mighty kings, princes, wise men, and dictators have come and gone but none lived, and ruled like our living God, who is eternal. He rules the earth. He is there everywhere. Man's thoughts are not God's thoughts. His ways are higher than ours. He is mightier than anyone. When man takes refuge in his own strength and wisdom the Lord will have him in derision.

The Father says He has set Jesus upon the holy hill of Zion. This is a prophecy and it is about the thousand year peaceful reign of our Lord Jesus Christ from the throne of David. The Father promises that the uttermost parts will be given to the Son for his possession. Jesus is the Son of God and he shall break the mighty men with iron rod and he breaks them as the rod strikes a potter's vessel. There were mighty men such as Sihon, king of Amoties, Og, the king of Bashaan, and Goliath in Philistine army but none prevailed against God and the children of Israel.

Sihon, king of the Amorites, opposed and tried to prevent in vain the Israelites to pass through his territory. The result was that he was defeated and Israelites not only took possession of his cities but they had their way through the land of Amorites. (Numbers 21:21-24)

Og, the king of Bashan, who was ruler over sixty cities, went out against Israelites but God assured Moses of his help and he defeated Og, the king of Bashan and took possession of his land. (Numbers 21:33-35)

There was a mighty man in Philistine army and his name was Goliath. David, a shepherd boy, son of Jessy, miraculously defeated the mighty Goliath, with the help of the Almighty God. David hurled one of his five smooth stones that he chose from the brook, from his sling that struck on the forehead of Goliath, who fell face down on the ground. David pulled out Goliath's sword from his sheath and killed him (cf. 1 Samuel 17:40-51)

"Therefore David ran, and stood upon the Philistine, and took his sword, and drew it out of the sheath thereof, and slew him, and cut off his head therewith. And when the Philistines saw their champion was dead, they fled" (1 Samuel 17:51)

There were other mighty men like Alexander the great, Napoleon, Hitler, etc. Some of them were great and some of them were very dangerous; but all of them died. Many dictators who stood strong defiantly in the recent past fell down and lost their eminent positions. Above all is our living God and His only begotten Son, Lord Jesus Christ is our Savior, who rule the earth. Is anyone now greater than these mighty men? If not, then let them know that everything is in our living God's control.

Psalmist points to antitype in Psalm Chapter 2 and exhorts, therefore, to serve Jesus with fear and rejoice. There is an interesting phrase used and it is "Kiss the Son". It is not an advice for us to kiss our sons but it is an exhortation to worship the Son of God, Lord Jesus Christ. It is very good that we kiss our sons, but here in this context it is not an exhortation to kiss our sons but it is an exhortation to worship the Son of God, Lord Jesus Christ. There is warning that if we do not worship the Son of God he would be angry and we may perish from the way. Psalmist says that those who put their trust in the Lord will be blessed.

Let us say as the children of Israel said when Joshua challenged them with a question as to whom they prefer to serve; whether it is idols or the living God! They all answered and said without any hesitation: "We will serve the LORD".

"And the people said unto Joshua, Nay; but we will serve the LORD". (Joshua 24:21)

PRAYER

Peter and John and their friends asserted that Herod, Pontius Pilate, Gentiles and the People of Israel gathered together and crucified Lord Jesus Christ and they did according as it was determined by the eternal counsel of the Almighty God. They pleaded with the LORD to grant them the boldness to counter the threatening, and courage to preach the Gospel of Jesus Christ. They prayed that the LORD may show signs and wonders. God answered their prayers and the place, where they assembled together shook; and they were all filled with Holy Spirit and spoke the word of God courageously. (cf. Acts 4:27-31)

"Jesus Christ the same yesterday, and to day, and for ever" (Hebrews 13:8). He knows what is happening and He is in control.

THE LESSONS

Peter and John, who preached the Gospel of Jesus Christ, did not do anything on their own accord, but they obeyed Lord Jesus Christ's instructions (Acts 1:8). They were great instruments in the hands of God, who used them to proclaim His Gospel. When Peter called upon the name of the Lord, and said to the lame man "In the name of Jesus Christ of Nazareth rise up and walk". A very noticeable point was that Peter, instead of claiming honor for him, repeatedly honored God by giving the Lord all the credit for healing the lame man.

AMID PERSECUTIONS

When the news of healing of the lame man went across the nation of Israel, and as they preached through Jesus the resurrection of the dead, the priests, the captain of the temple, and the Sadducees felt grieved and jealous and took Peter and John into custody. It being the evening, they held them till the next morning.

The next day, they set Peter and John before their rulers, elders, scribes, Annas the high priest and Caiaphas, and John and Alexander, and before all the kindred of the high priest. The authorities questioned them by what power or by what name they were preaching the resurrection of Jesus they and healed the lame man. Sadducees never believed in resurrection. However, Peter filled, with Holy Spirit boldly, stood witness for Lord Jesus Christ.

"But Peter and John answered and said unto them, Whether it be right in the sight of God to hearken unto you more than unto God, judge ye. For we cannot but speak the things which we have seen and heard" (Acts 4:19-20)

The rulers, and all other authorities, who were trying to send Peter and John to Jail for a term, feared the crowd, who saw the miracle happen, and the man standing before them live with perfect legs. Peter reiterated that the man was healed by the power of Lord Jesus Christ, whom they crucified on the cross, and whom the death could not hold Him in the grave. God raised Jesus from the dead on the third day, and the Lord ascended into heaven after forty days.

There is another point of interest that we need to take note of here is that it is not only Jews who were responsible for the crucifixion of Jesus, Gentiles as well. It was Herod, who was an Edomite, a descendant from Esau's lineage, mocked Jesus and sent Him back to Pilate without acquitting Him or giving orders to Pilate the Governor to acquit Him of all the false charges levelled against Him. It was Pilate, who was a Gentile, wrote the death sentence on Jesus and condemned the Lord to be crucified on the cross.

"For of a truth against thy holy child Jesus, whom thou hast anointed, both Herod, and Pontius Pilate, with the Gentiles, and the people of Israel, were gathered together" (Acts 4:27)

This was the first persecution in a series of persecutions that were going to come; and it was all successful ending for the servants of God, who preached the Gospel of Lord Jesus Christ. The authorities could not do any harm to Peter and John, the servants of God and, therefore, released them from the custody. History shows us that this is what has been happening all through, and the Truth prevails upon the falsehood and persecution.

Peter and John did not keep quiet after being released from the custody but they went to their company of friends and reported to them all that happened to them and the ill-treatment they encountered from the authorities. The earth shook and Holy Spirit came upon them as they and their friends all together prayed with one accord and praised God. Later, they all spoke the Word of God boldly.

"And when they had prayed, the place was shaken where they were assembled together; and they were all filled with the Holy Ghost, and they spake the word of God with boldness" (Acts 4:31)

When Shadrach, Meshach, and Abednego were thrown into the hot furnace of fire, they were not all alone, but the

Christophany (the presence of Christ) was with them, and King Nebuchadnezzar saw four persons in the burning furnace (cf. Daniel 3:19-26).

"Then Nebuchadnezzar the king was astonied, and rose up in haste, and spake, and said unto his counsellors, Did not we cast three men bound into the midst of the fire? They answered and said unto the king, True, O king. He answered and said, Lo, I see four men loose, walking in the midst of the fire, and they have no hurt; and the form of the fourth is like the Son of God" (Daniel 3:24-25)

When Daniel was thrown into the den of lions, the mouths of the lions were shut by God. When King Darius questioned him as to how he was saved Daniel replied saying...

"Then said Daniel unto the king, O king, live for ever. My God hath sent his angel, and hath shut the lions' mouths, that they have not hurt me: forasmuch as before him innocency was found in me; and also before thee, O king, have I done no hurt" (Daniel 6:21-22)

Persecution never prevails over the Truth. It may temporarily appear as if persecution prevailed, but in all cases of persecution, the Church grew. God knows whether the flesh and blood of those who were persecuted really felt the pain.

Man by his own strength cannot survive persecution nor can he withstand the pain inflicted on him but believer can hope in the Lord that as he suffers persecution God delivers him from the suffering. Jesus said:

"And fear not them which kill the body, but are not able to kill the soul: but rather fear him which is able to destroy both soul and body in hell" (Matthew 10:28)

CHAPTER 13
THE SECOND PERSECUTION

ANANIAS AND SAPPHIRA

After the first persecution ended, the apostles were allowed to go scot-free. Apostles praised God and proclaimed the Gospel of Jesus Christ with one accord and in one soul. During this period they in all their enthusiasm to serve the Lord, considered their finances as for common use, yet not for improper use as anyone desired. The contributor had the privileges of giving as much from their personal finances as another was in need.

As for sharing finances there were two examples cited; one of Joses, who was later called Barnabas, the meaning of which was a son of encouragement. He was a Levite, who sold his property and brought entire amount and placed it at the feet of the apostles for use as apostles decided; and another of Ananias and his wife Sapphira, who sold their possessions and subtly kept back a portion of their money and brought to the apostles as if they gave the entire amount. They showed hypocrisy in their offering and lied to Peter that they brought entire money to the apostles.

Peter, who was filled with Holy Spirit sensed their hypocrisy, questioned Ananias first if he had brought entire money from their sold property. Ananias lied to Peter that he did and was, therefore, instantly died. After an interval of three hours Sapphira came by them and when she was questioned if they had brought the entire money, she lied just as her husband did to Peter and she died instantly, as well.

Ananias and Sapphira died instantly one after another for lying to the Holy Spirit. Their death was not because they did not give their entire income, but because they lied to the Holy Spirit. They pretended as if they gave their entire income while they did not indeed.

Peter questioned them if the money that they brought to the feet of apostles was not theirs when the possessions were sold, and if it was not within their freedom to bring as much as they could offer, but inasmuch as they lied to him and to the Holy Spirit, he pronounced a harsh punishment on them, and therefore, Ananias and Sapphira faced instant death.

It may be recalled that Lord Jesus gave him power that whatever he binds on the earth it will be bound in heaven, and whatever he loose on the earth, it will be loosened in heaven (cf. Matthew 16:19).

The wages of sin is death in all cases; however in the early days of Church history they faced instant wrath from God; that was a different age than of ours. We are under grace and are forgiven instantly if we confess our sins to the Lord by faith in Him.

"Moreover the law entered, that the offence might abound. But where sin abounded, grace did much more abound" (Romans 5:20)

It was a time, when the Church was growing and there were numerous miracles done. The miracles done by the Apostles were so numerous that people with sickness waited for the shadows of them to fall on them and as many as came under their shadows were all healed.

APOSTLES ARRESTED

The high priest and the Sadducees, being filled with rage and indignation at the preaching and the healing by the Apostles, arrested them and lodged them in common prison. Jesus predicted much before His death that that His followers will face such persecutions and said in such circumstances, as Peter and others faced, they do not need to worry about but depend on Holy Spirit, who will teach them as to what they should speak and do.

"And when they bring you unto the synagogues, and unto magistrates, and powers, take ye no thought how or what thing ye shall answer, or what ye shall say: For the Holy Ghost shall teach you in the same hour what ye ought to say" (Luke 12:11-12)

"But before all these, they shall lay their hands on you, and persecute you, delivering you up to the synagogues, and into prisons, being brought before kings and rulers for my name's sake" (Luke 21:12)

But before all these, they shall lay their hands on you, and persecute you, delivering you up to the synagogues, and into prisons, being brought before kings and rulers for my name's sake. (Luke 21:12)

They felt jealousy towards the apostles because many people were gathering around them to listen to the truth. The secular authorities rejected the truth and instead followed the falsehood. Bible tells us to seek the truth and discard the falsehood even if it appears to be good to embrace.

"But if you have bitter jealousy and selfish ambition in your hearts, do not boast and be false to the truth" (James 3:14 ESV)

ANGEL OF THE LORD RESCUES

However, the angel of the Lord came to their rescue and opened the prison doors and after bringing them out of the prison said to them to go and preach to the people the Gospel of Jesus Christ in the temple.

The high priest called for the council and the senate of the children of Israel and demanded that the apostles be brought before them, in order that the council may reach a consensual agreement to sentence apostles for a term in the prison. However, when they went to bring them from the common prison they did not find them there.

The officers solemnly affirmed that they had lodged the apostles in the prison and secured them with all the possible best safety methods besides keepers standing before the doors. To their surprise they did not find anyone inside when they opened the gates.

The high priest and the captain of the temple and the chief priests did not believe that such miracle could happen. In the meanwhile there came a man and told them that those who were lodged in the common prison were standing in the temple and teaching the people.

On hearing the news the captain along with other officers went and brought them without exhibiting any violence because they feared the people. The people, who were witnesses of many miracles from the apostles, were on their side, and therefore, the authorities feared that they would be stoned if they behaved violently against the Apostles.

They brought them and set them before the council and then there came out a sharp question from the mouth of high priest who asked them if he and his colleagues did not ask them not to teach in the name of Jesus. They alleged that the Apostles filled Jerusalem with their doctrine and intended the blood of Jesus to come upon them.

APOSTLES RESIST THE COUNCIL

Peter and other apostles answered firmly in the midst of persecution that they had to obey God rather than men. They proclaimed that Jesus, whom they crucified on the cross, was raised from the dead and exalted by God with His right hand to be a Prince and Savior to give repentance to Israel and forgiveness of sins. They said they are witnesses of these things, and so is also the Holy Spirit, whom God gave to them to obey Him.

The authorities heard the explanations of apostles and as to how the apostles were delivered by the angel of the Lord from persecution, and therefore, they were all in consensus to kill them. It is at that time that God intervened by sending a Pharisee named Gamaliel, who was doctor of the Law, and had very good reputation among all the people to speak to secular authorities. He commanded them to give a short break before they arbitrarily judged to punish the apostles.

GAMALIEL CITES THEUDAS AND JUDAS

Gamaliel spoke and said if their proclamation of the Gospel was true and if it was allowed by God the teaching will sustain; otherwise they and their message will be brought to naught.

He cited two examples of fake ministers, namely, Theudas and Judas, who boasted that they were true messengers of God and they needed to be accepted. He brought to their notice how Theudas, who had about four hundred followers, was slain and his followers scattered beyond any recognition. He also brought to their notice of Judas of Galilee, who drew great number of men as his followers, probably luring them by providing tax benefits, but perished, and as many as those followed him were dispersed.

Therefore, Gamaliel, Doctor of Law pursued them they should refrain from punishing the apostles and let them alone. He assured them that if the work of the apostles is of God they cannot overthrow them or their work, otherwise they will be in danger of fighting with God. Bible says no wisdom, or any understanding or any counsel can stand against the LORD.

There is no wisdom nor understanding nor counsel against the LORD. (Proverbs 21:30)

The high priest and the chief priests and others who had earlier decided to punish apostles let them go after allowing them to be beaten up. Before allow them to go they commanded that they should not speak in the name of Jesus but the apostles departed from the council, rejoicing and counting their persecution as worthy to suffer shame for the name of Lord Jesus Christ. Thereafter, they did not cease to preach the Gospel of Jesus Christ daily in the temple and in every house.

CHAPTER 14
THE THIRD PERSECUTION

STEPHEN STANDS FOR JESUS

In the early days after the ascension of Lord Jesus Christ, when Apostles started working for the proclamation of Gospel of Jesus Christ the power of God was clearly seen when multitude of people were saved. In Acts Chapter 2 this fact is seen. Apostle Peter spoke about repentance and there were three thousand souls added to those who were already saved. And they continued steadfastly in the "apostles' doctrine and fellowship, and in breaking of bread, and in prayers". (Acts 2:42)

The Church grew and the disciples were of the view that they should devote more time and energy for the purpose of serving God rather than pursuing secular interests. It was then that they took a decision to appoint seven men with honest report, filled with Holy Spirit and with the wisdom to do this job. Their decision was in consequence to their willingness to dedicate their entire time and energy for prayer and for the ministry of the Word of God.

Seven men they chose for this work as recorded in Acts 6:5 were "Stephen, a man full of faith and of the Holy Ghost, and Philip, and Prochorus, and Nicanor, and Timon, and Parmenas, and Nicolas a proselyte of Antioch". Of the seven men chosen Stephen deserves more of our attention than others.

Stephen was full of faith and power. Few people rose up against him from the synagogue, which was the synagogue of the Libertines, Cyrenians, and Alexandrians and of them of Cilicia and of Asia disputing with him as he did great wonders and miracles among the people and spoke about Jesus.

Unable to resist the wisdom and the spirit by which he spoke they accused him of speaking against the Law of Moses and against God. They stirred up elders, the scribes and brought false witnesses. They accused Stephen saying that he spoke of Jesus of Nazareth that he would destroy their place. Then the high priest asked Stephen if the charges leveled against him were true.

Stephen spoke in defense of the atoning sacrifice of Lord Jesus Christ. He brought home an important point in his defense that the people, elders and the scribes, who alleged him of blaspheming God and promoting violation of Moses law, were as much stiff necked people in their beliefs and refusing to accept Messiah as their Savior, as the children of Israel did by worshipping idols during Moses' period.

Stephen calls them, 'ye stiff necked people'. This phrase was used by God earlier in the Old Testament against the children of Israel, who defied the LORD's love and care for them. They preferred worshipping idols rather than worshipping the living God. Aaron, who was supposed to guard them against all such evil practices, took a leading role in making a molten calf and worshipping it in preference to the living God. They insulted the LORD who brought them out from the bondage of slavery under Pharaoh.

The high priest, before whom Stephen was testifying about the love of Lord Jesus Christ, was jealous of the miracles and wonders Stephen was doing in the name of Lord Jesus Christ. The high priest was afraid that if Stephen continued to glorify God by speaking boldly about him with great faith his own position would be at stakes. These high priests, Annas, before him Peter and John stood, and Caiaphas, before whom Jesus stood, were not the kind of high priests who were of the order from Aaron and his sons, but these were usurpers of power, strength and position. Their main aim was to see that their own position was secure.

Stephen, therefore, calls them "Ye stiff-necked", and said that they always resisted the Holy Spirit just as their fathers did in the wilderness. He questioned them as to which prophet escaped their persecution and concluded that they followed their own understanding and rejected Jesus Christ. They took pride that they were circumcised. Stephen, therefore, says:

"Ye stiffnecked and uncircumcised in heart and ears, ye do always resist the Holy Ghost: as your fathers did, so do ye. Which of the prophets have not your fathers persecuted? and they have slain them which shewed before of the coming of the Just One; of whom ye have been now the betrayers and murderers". (Acts 7:51, 52)

"And they stoned Stephen, calling upon God, and saying, Lord Jesus, receive my spirit" (Acts 7:59)

While breathing his last, Stephen knelt down and "cried with a loud voice", and said "Lord, lay not this sin to their charge. And when he had said this, he fell asleep". (Ref: Acts 7:60)

Stephen was the first martyr who gave up his mortal life for the sake of proclaiming the saving grace of Lord Jesus Christ, who was the Son of God. Jesus came into this world for taking upon him our sins and die on behalf of us, in order that whoever believes on him shall not perish but have everlasting life. The people stoned Stephen to death for standing for Jesus Christ.

Jesus said: "Blessed are ye, when men shall revile you, and persecute you, and shall say all manner of evil against you falsely, for my sake. Rejoice, and be exceeding glad: for great is your reward in heaven: for so persecuted they the prophets which were before you". (Matthew 5:11-12)

"Then said Jesus, Father, forgive them; for they know not what they do. And they parted his raiment, and cast lots" (Luke 23:34)

STEPHEN GLORIFIES GOD

"And Stephen, full of faith and power, did great wonders and miracles among the people" (Acts 6:8)

The life of Stephen recorded in the Bible draws our attention to the fact that he was full of faith and power. The high priest was jealous of hearing about the miracles and wonders that Stephen did with great power and faith in Jesus.

Those who were against Stephen's stand for Jesus rose up against him disputing with him but could not resist the wisdom and the spirit that was in him by which he did miracles and wonders. Those who determined to work against Stephen were accusing him falsely that he was speaking blasphemy against Moses and their God.

They caused emotional stir up among people and brought Stephen before the council for a trial. Even as they laid false charge against Stephen that he said Jesus of Nazareth shall destroy that place, and would change the customs of Moses gave to them, they saw that the face of Stephen was shining like that of an angel. (Acts 6:8-15)

AMID PERSECUTIONS

The high priest who was more or like the mouth of the court asked Stephen if he was speaking blasphemy against their God and was working to see that the customs of Moses were changed.

Stephen full of power and grace from God spoke elaborately outwitting the knowledge of the high priest. The elders, scribes and the people brought him to stand before high priest to face the false charges lodged against him.

Stephen defended by speaking about Abraham with whom God made covenant and explained in detail about the Almighty God, who dwelt not in the temples made with hands but whose throne is Heaven, and whose footstool is the earth. He spoke about the God of Israel who delivered the children of Israel from the bondage of slavery and he spoke about Moses whom God had appointed as the leader to stand boldly before Pharaoh. He spoke of about Joseph whom God had sent ahead of his parents and his brethren to Egypt to find sustenance for them before there came great famine in the land of Egypt and Canaan.

Stephen gave the God of Israel the glory due unto His name. He did not speak blasphemy but recognized the protection the Lord gave to His children. He spoke of the mighty power of God that humbled all his enemies and the enemies of the children of Israel. He did not speak a word against Lord Jesus Christ; rather he gave glory unto name of Lord Jesus Christ. As the people stoned him he called upon Lord Jesus Christ and prayed to receive his spirit. And, even as he was breathing his last, he said, 'lay not this sin to their charge'.

"And they stoned Stephen, calling upon God, and saying, Lord Jesus, receive my spirit. And he kneeled down, and cried with a loud voice, Lord, lay not this sin to their charge. And when he had said this, he fell asleep". (Acts 7:59-60)

CHAPTER 15
THE FOURTH PERSECUTION

SAUL PERSECUTES THE CHURCH

Apostle Paul, who was known by the name Saul before his conversion to Christianity, said he had much grudge and hatred toward Christians and their beliefs.

Therefore, he decided to do many things contrary to the name of Lord Jesus Christ of Nazareth. He had shut up many Christians in prisons with the authority that he received from the chief priests and voiced against them when they were put to death.

He punished believers in synagogue and compelled them to blaspheme Christ. His hatred towards Christians was so great that he persecuted them in even in unknown cities. Moreover, he obtained letter of authority from chief priest and was going to Damascus to execute his purpose.

Paul's addressing excels anybody's expectations that even in such a great disadvantageous position as prisoner as he was he exclaims with much emotion "At midday, O king" and then proceeds. The way he addresses is so pleasing...

"At midday, O king, I saw in the way a light from heaven, above the brightness of the sun, shining round about me and them which journeyed with me" (Acts 26:13)

Paul's addressing next is again so pleasing...

"Whereupon, O king Agrippa, I was not disobedient unto the heavenly vision" (Acts 26:19)

Paul was speaking about his conversion. He narrates as to how a great light from heaven shone around midday and Paul and all those who accompanied him fell down to the ground. Only Paul heard a voice in Hebrew tongue from heaven that questioned him "Saul,. Saul why persecutest me? It is hard for you to kick against pricks"

Then Paul cried out saying "Who art thou Lord?" and the voice said "I am Jesus whom thou persecutest".

But the voice from Lord Jesus Christ comforted Paul and said that he was chosen vessel to minister the word of God and be a witness for Him of all that he has seen and would see in future. Lord Jesus Christ sent Paul specifically to carry His Gospel to the Gentiles.

Paul said to King Agrippa that he was not disobedient to the vision and command that he received from heaven. He preached Gospel of Jesus Christ at Damascus, at Jerusalem, at Judea and Samaria and then in uttermost parts of the earth to the Gentiles.

The message he carried was that those who hear the Gospel of Jesus Christ should repent of their sins to Lord Jesus Christ and receive salvation. This was the reason why Paul was caught by Jews in the temple and attempts were made by them to kill him. As he obtained command and help from God he continued preaching none other beliefs than that the prophets and Moses spoke of. He preached that Christ who was spoken of by prophets needs to have come, die for the sins of mankind and be the first among the resurrected. He preached that Christ suffered death and showed light unto the Gentiles as also to the Jews.

APOSTLE PAUL TURNS TO GENTILES

Acts Chapter 13 has details about Apostle Paul's endeavors to turn Jews from their obstinate stance of rejection of Jesus as their Messiah. He details great many events that have taken place in the past right from the days of Abraham until the resurrection of Jesus.

Paul tried to convey the message of salvation that is available only in Lord Jesus Christ but Jews not only stirred up the devout and honorable women and the chief men of the Antioch, but also persecuted Paul and Barnabas. They expelled them from their region. As Lord Jesus Christ commanded his disciples to shake off the dust against that city and go ahead to another city (Matthew 10:14)

Paul and Barnabas followed the example and they shook off the dust off their feet against them. The disciples were filled with joy and with the Holy Spirit.

It started when the CHURCH at Antioch had prophets and teachers among who were four names were prominent. They were: (1) Barnabas (2) Simeon who was also called Niger (3) Lucius of Cyrene and (4) Manaen.

The Holy Spirit separated Paul and Barnabas for working for Lord Jesus Christ. The Church laid hands on Paul and Barnabas and sent them for work. This was a follow up of what Lord Jesus wanted from Paul. Lord Jesus Christ called Saul and said about him that "...he is a chosen vessel unto me, to bear my name before the Gentiles, and kings, and the children of Israel" (Acts 9:15) Saul was called by the name Paul.

AMID PERSECUTIONS

This was the beginning of the ministry by Paul first to the Jews and then to the Gentiles. Earlier Peter spoke to the men of Israel (Ref. Acts Chapters 1 and 2). The early ministry of Paul and Barnabas was not an easy one. They were sent out into the midst of powerful unbelieving men of Israel and then to the Gentiles. The Church and the Ministry was in the beginning stages. As they were traveling from Selucia and from there to Cyprus they encountered many hardships.

One of the toughest encounters they faced was with a sorcerer, who was a Jew and a false prophet, whose name was Barjesus. After dealing with this sorcerer they had another sorcerer come in their way and his name was Elymas, who opposed preaching of the Gospel of Jesus Christ.

When they were at Salamis they preached the word of God in the SYNAGOGUES of the Jews. Paul and Barnabas had John also with them for working for the Lord. While they were passing through that isle to Paphos, they came across Barjesus, who was with the deputy of the country, Sergius Paulus.

Sergius was a wise man and he called Paul and Barnabas and desired to hear the word of God from them. Elymas opposed preaching of the word of God to Sergius Paulus thinking that Sergius would turn away from his faith. Paul filled with the Holy Spirit set his eyes on Elymas and said to him...

"O full of all subtilty and all mischief, thou child of the devil, thou enemy of all righteousness, wilt thou not cease to pervert the right ways of the Lord? And now, behold, the hand of the Lord is upon thee, and thou shalt be blind, not seeing the sun for a season" (Acts 13:10)

Elymas lost sight "for a season" because of the curse and seeing this deputy Sergius Paulus believed in the Lord.

From Paphos Paul, Barnabas and John went to Perga in Pemphylia. From there John departed from then and returned to Jerusalem. Paul and Barnabas departed from Perga and came to Antioth in Pisidia and went to SYNAGOGUE on the Sabbath day and sat down. The rulers of the SYNAGOGUE sent unto them to speak if they have anything to speak about the law, prophets.

Paul then stood and addressed them as "Men of Israel, and ye that fear God, give audience."

Paul went on describing in detail as to how God of the people of Israel chose the patriarchs and exalted them when they were as strangers in the land of Egypt.

With great might God delivered them from the bondage under Pharaoh. God destroyed seven nations when they were on their journey from Egypt to Canaan. God gave to them Judges to guide them in the way of the Lord for four hundred and fifty years until Samuel the prophet. But then they desired to have a king to rule over them.

God gave Saul the son of Cis, one who was of the tribe of Benjamin, for forty years. God removed him and raised up unto them David to be their king and the Lord himself said that he found David, the son of Jesse as a man after his own heart and that he will fulfill His will. God raised up from the seed of David a Savior unto Israel and his name was Jesus.

John the Baptist preached the repentance by Baptism to all the people of Israel. John said he was not worthy to lose the latchet of the One who comes after him. Paul says that the salvation was sent out to the men and brethren, children of the stock of Abraham, and whosoever fears God.

Every Sabbath day these men of Jerusalem and their rulers who read in the SYNAGOGUES the law and prophet did not yet believe on Jesus but condemned him. They found no reason to kill Jesus, yet they desired of Pilate the Jesus should be slain. When they had fulfilled everything that was written of him they took him down from the cross and laid in a sepulcher. But God raised him from the dead. Jesus was seen by many during those days and Paul says Paul and his Barnabas were witnesses to these events.

Paul tells the audience that Jesus the Messiah had come as prophesied (Psalm Chapter 2:7) and God raised him from the dead and he will have sure mercies of David. Even as David saw corruption and was laid to rest along with his fathers, no one could see corruption in Jesus. This was also in fulfillment of prophesying as prophesied. (Psalms 16:10) Paul then declares that through the Son of man was preached the forgiveness of sins. He declares that all those who believe him are justified from all things from which they could not be justified by the law of Moses.

Prophet Habakkuk had burden for the children of Israel that they were going away from the Lord and slack in following the commandments of the Lord. The prophet cries out to God showing his concern for them and says how long these people would go unpunished for their wickedness and iniquity.

The Lord says that he would raise up Chaldeans against them and scatter them. God warned about this in earlier as we read in Deuteronomy 28:64-67. As per the word of God they were scattered and God says that he will do the work that they do not believe even if they were told about it. Paul quotes this verse in his speech and warns Jews about their disbelief and rejection of Jesus as their Messiah.

Behold ye among the heathen, and regard, and wonder marvellously: for I will work a work in your days, which ye will not believe, though it be told you. (Habakkuk 1:5)

As prophesied earlier the Jews did neither accept Jesus as their Messiah nor did Apostle Paul as one sent to preach the gospel of Jesus Christ. The Gentiles came in when they saw that Jews left from the SYNAGOGUE and requested Paul and Barnabas to preach to them the same message that they spoke to the Jews the next Sabbath day.

Congregation was divided over this issue and may Jews and religious proselyte followed Paul and Barnabas. Paul and Barnabas advised all of them to continue in the grace of God. Almost the whole city came together to hear the word of God from Paul and Barnabas the next Sabbath day. But the envy in Jews grew more when they saw the multitudes following Paul and Barnabas and spoke against them and said to the multitude that Paul and Barnabas were contradicting and blaspheming.

It was then that Paul and Barnabas became bold and said that it was necessary that the word of God should have been first spoken to the Jews and admonished that they were not worthy of everlasting life. It was then that they turned to the Gentiles. It was then that Paul said that he was set apart to take the Gospel of Jesus Christ and the message of salvation to the Gentiles unto the ends of the earth.

When the Gentiles heard these words from Apostle Paul they were glad and glorified the word of the Lord and as many as were elected by God unto eternal life believed. The word of the Lord was published the entire region. When the Jews expelled them they shook off the dust off their feet and went to Iconium. (Acts 13:40-52)

CHAPTER 16
THE FIFTH PERSECUTION

PETER RESCUED

In order to understand the cruel nature of Herod's it is necessary to know how they were prominent during Biblical times. They were Edomites from the lineage of Esau.

Herod Agrippa was the grandson of Herod the great, who ordered killing of male children of less than two years of age, during the time when Jesus was born, in order to ensure that Jesus was killed (Matt 2:1; 2:16). His plans were foiled. Herod Aristobulus was the son of Herod the great, and Herod Agrippa was the son of Aristobulus, who was the nephew of Herod Antipas. Herod Agrippa killed Herod Aristobulus, and Herod Antipas ordered beheading of John the Baptist. Herod Agrippa II, before whom Paul stood for trial, was the son of Herod Agrippa (Ref. Antiquities of the Jews - Book XVIII Chapter 5).

Herod Agrippa stretched forth his hands as a sign of his approval to persecute the Church (cf. Acts 12:1). Stretching forth of hands denotes approval. He was the one who killed James the brother of John with the sword.

It pleased the Jews, during the early days of the growth of the Church, to persecute those who worked for Lord Jesus Christ. James the brother of John was one who suffered persecution and was killed by the sword of Herod. When Herod came to know that the death of James pleased Jews he went one step ahead and apprehended Peter and put him in prison. Those were the days of feast of "unleavened bread".

AMID PERSECUTIONS

Herod employed sixteen soldiers as guards to keep a watch over Peter that he may not escape from the prison. His intention was to bring Peter before the people after the following Easter.

Now, when Peter was under custody in prison, under the supervision of so powerful guard as of sixteen soldiers, the church prayed to God for him. Peter was sleeping between two soldiers on the night before he was scheduled to be brought before the people. He was bound with two chains and keepers guarded the door of the prison.

In the midst of so much human security guarding Peter, an angel of the Lord came to him, and shone light to him in the prison. As Peter was comfortably sleeping the angel of the Lord smote Peter on the side to wake him up from sleep and when he woke up the angel said to him to arise quickly. As the chains fell off from Peter's hands he obeyed the instructions of the angel of the Lord, who said to him to gird up and wear sandals. As the angel of the Lord instructed he wore garment around him and followed him. As these things were happening Peter did not think that it was real; but thought it was a vision.

When they passed two wards and came to the Iron Gate that leads to the city the gate opened to them, without any human intervention, and they went out. The angel departed after Peter passed comfortably through the first street. As Peter was walking alone he realized that the Lord sent His angel and delivered him from out of the hand of Herod, and from all the expectations of Jews, who were in favor of killing him.

RHODA'S BELIEF

By the time Peter realized that it was not a dream but was real he was at the house of Mary the mother of John, whose surname was Mark. There were many who gathered in that house for praying and as Peter knocked at the door of the house a young woman named Rhoda came to the door and heard the voice of Peter. She was so confident that the voice was of Peter that she ran into the house, instead of opening the door, and announced to all those who were praying for Peter that her was standing at the door. She heard the voice of Peter and believed it to be of him, while after hearing the announcement they, who were praying, chastised her saying she was mad. However, as she constantly insisted in saying that the voice was of Peter, they said he could be angel of Peter. (Rhoda was the same girl who pointed Peter and questioned him, at the time of Lord Jesus's crucifixion, if he was not one of the disciples of Jesus; and Peter had firmly denied. Later when Jesus looked at him he repented of his denial).

PRAYER ANSWERED

The prayer of the Church was answered and Peter was there at their door; and yet they had questions if the man knocking the door was really Peter. Peter's incessant knocking of the door resulted in their change of mind, and they opened the door and to their surprise they saw it was truly Peter. Perhaps, they were scared, as human as we are, of the persecutions by the soldiers and Herod's followers. They were reluctant to open the door; but later when they opened the door; they saw and believed what seemed to have been an unbelievable an incident.

Peter showed a sign to them and proclaimed as to how the Lord brought him out of the prison. After narrating to James and to the brethren the things that have happened, Peter departed and went to another place.

According to Roman law, during the days of apostles, the soldiers who kept charge of the prisoners were responsible ensure that the prisoners do not escape from the prison; otherwise, they were subjected to the punishment that the prisoner would have received. Here, when Peter was delivered miraculously by the angel, the guarding soldiers did not know as to how it all happened. That is the reason why there was great furor among them and they were all in great fear.

SOLDIERS EXECUTED

Herod interrogated the guarding soldiers, who had no convincing reply for Herod to pardon them and, therefore, he ordered them to be executed to death.

Peter, who was rescued from out of the prison by the angel of the Lord, went down from Judaea to Caesarea and lived there.

It is interesting to see that God allowed James to die with the sword of Herod but He delivered Peter from the hand of Herod. Who could question the Sovereign God of His actions? The Lord knows who is to stay on in this world for a longer period and who is not to. It is the Lord's will that prevailed.

When it was time for James, half-brother of Jesus, was to be called Home, he was gone, after being a pillar in the house of the Lord, ministering for the growth of the Church. When Jesus was on this earth James refused to be a believer in Him, and after the death of Jesus he insisted on seeing the risen Jesus Christ in order to accept Him as the Lord. Paul writes in 1 Corinthians 15:7 that James saw the risen Lord. Thereafter, the half-brothers of Lord Jesus Christ, James and John, became strong pillars in the building of the Church.

Herod was angry on cities namely, Tyre and Sidon, for unknown reason, but because these cities were dependent on Herod for their supplies of food etc., made friendship with Blastus, who was officer in charge of a chamber in King's palace.

HEROD KILLED

On a certain day when Herod, in his royal apparel, sat on his throne and made a public speech the people applauded him. They went beyond a simple applause to say that his voice was of a god, and not of a man. At this juncture, Herod should have replied to them that he was not a god, nor was an angel to say the least, inasmuch as not even angels were not supposed to receive worship from men. Instead, Herod accepted the saying of the people that he was a god, and therefore, the angel of the Lord smote him, and he was eaten of worms and died.

THE CHURCH GREW

The word of God spread and multiplied and the church grew strong. An important mention is made here, of Barnabas and Saul returning from Jerusalem, and that after they had fulfilling their ministry, they took with them John, whose surname was Mark, the writer of the Gospel of Mark. In the ensuring chapters of Acts of Apostles it can be seen how church grew.

CHAPTER 17
VENGEANCE BELONGS TO GOD

"Give ear to my words, O LORD, consider my meditation. Hearken unto the voice of my cry, my King, and my God: for unto thee will I pray" Psalm 5:1-2

In his Psalm 5, David seeks God's ears to hear his words and pleads that his petition may be heard. Calling God as His king, David addresses his prayer to none but pointedly to Him alone, and pleads that his cry may be heard.

David was sure that Jehovah, who made him king over Israel, will hear his morning prayer because he directs it to none else but to Him alone. He looks up to the living God, who chose him as king over Israel. He directs his prayer to God of his fathers because He takes no pleasure in wickedness nor does He allow any evil to dwell near Him. God detests every worker of iniquity, and therefore, He takes no pleasure in any of those evil workers and they will never be able to stand in His sight.

God abhors gossipers and destroys those who speak vanity. He abhors those who seek to shed blood of others and deceive men. But as for David, he promises God that He will come into the His house to worship Him looking towards His holy temple, in awe and fear, and enter into multitude of His mercies. His wish was that God may look at him.

God is faithful and just and His mercies will never fail. He is slow to anger and longsuffering. However, as for the enemies of David, he says, there is no faithfulness in their mouths when they speak, and their hearts are highly wicked. Their throats, he says, are like open sepulcher, and they flatter with selfish motives to achieve their own selfish purposes.

David, as a king facing challenging situations, and with complex problems to rule the nation of Israel, prays to God to destroy the evil ones that they may fall by their own counsels. Considering that his enemies rebelled against God, he seeks God to cast them out because of their huge number of transgressions. He commits evil doers and his enemies to God to take action. Vengeance belongs to God.

"To me belongeth vengeance and recompence; their foot shall slide in due time: for the day of their calamity is at hand, and the things that shall come upon them make haste" Deuteronomy 32:35

He prays for those who put their trust in the LORD that they may rejoice in Him and shout praises to him in joy because God defends them. His desire is that they may love the LORD and joyful in Him.

However, he is confident that the LORD God of Israel, Jehovah, will bless the righteous with favor and cover them with His shield.

If David depended on God for action against his enemies, then how much more we should depend on Him to help us out from troubles and problems!

Man has to put in his utmost skills to take vengeance against his aggressors and many times he gets defeated in the process.

It is because man does not trust God that He can take care of our problems that man devises plans and strategies to take vengeance on those who are aggressors.

Trust in the Lord that He is capable of taking vengeance. God says "vengeance in mine".

Christianity preaches peace; it is a relationship with God. Bible says:

"Blessed are they which are persecuted for righteousness' sake: for theirs is the kingdom of heaven. Blessed are ye, when men shall revile you, and persecute you, and shall say all manner of evil against you falsely, for my sake. Rejoice, and be exceeding glad: for great is your reward in heaven: for so persecuted they the prophets which were before you" (Matthew 5:10-12)

"But I say unto you, Love your enemies, bless them that curse you, do good to them that hate you, and pray for them which despitefully use you, and persecute you; That ye may be the children of your Father which is in heaven: for he maketh his sun to rise on the evil and on the good, and sendeth rain on the just and on the unjust" (Matthew 5:44-45)

"Dearly beloved, avenge not yourselves, but rather give place unto wrath: for it is written, Vengeance is mine; I will repay, saith the Lord" Romans 12:19.

CHAPTER 18
VENGEANCE IS NOT TOO FAR

From Revelation 6:9-11

"When he opened the fifth seal, I saw under the altar the souls of those who had been slain for the word of God and for the witness they had borne. They cried out with a loud voice, "O Sovereign Lord, holy and true, how long before you will judge and avenge our blood on those who dwell on the earth?" Then they were each given a white robe and told to rest a little longer, until the number of their fellow servants and their brothers should be complete, who were to be killed as they themselves had been" (Revelation 6:9-11 ESV")

A notable feature that needs our cognizance is that when the fifth seal is opened there was no announcement from any of the four living creatures of the impending events that would come to pass. Instead, John saw the souls of those saints who were persecuted and killed for the word of God and bearing witness for the Lord.

The souls of those killed for standing for the Lord may have been there under the altar for quite a great deal of time. However, they knew that the Lord would avenge their blood on those who dwell on the earth, but did not know how long it would take. Rather, in their impatience they seek an answer from the Sovereign Lord.

The Lord said to them that they should wait until the number of martyrs for Him is complete with those fellow servants and their brothers who would die, just as they were persecuted and killed. Each soul under the altar was given a white robe. The answer is found in Revelation 7:14 where one of the elders said they, and the rest of the ones killed later as martyrs for the Lord, during "great tribulation", came out and had "washed their robes, and made them white in the blood of the Lamb"

It is but natural for human beings to cry to the Lord, when their enemies are still in good life enjoying the pleasures of life. When Psalmist was in much agony he cried to the LORD this way several times. The cry of the souls, which are under the altar, to the Lord was similar. They sought vengeance by the Lord, as soon as possible, not knowing God's purposes.

"O Lord, how long shall the wicked, how long shall the wicked exult?" Psalm 94:3

"How long, O Lord? Will you hide yourself forever? How long will your wrath burn like fire?" Psalm 89:46

The souls under the altar were of those who stood for the Lord during "great tribulation" and had neither worshipped Antichrist or his image nor received the "mark of the beast" on their foreheads or their hands. They came to life with Christ to reign with Him for a thousand years.

"Then I saw thrones, and seated on them were those to whom the authority to judge was committed. Also I saw the souls of those who had been beheaded for the testimony of Jesus and for the word of God, and those who had not worshiped the beast or its image and had not received its mark on their foreheads or their hands. They came to life and reigned with Christ for a thousand years" (Revelation 20:4

There are few interesting points to take note of. The souls were under the altar. The temple was already destroyed in AD 70, before John wrote Revelation in about AD 96, and therefore, this is surely a vision, alluding to the brazen altar, where the sacrifices and prayers were offered by priests, and which was outside the Tabernacle, or Temple of God. The other altar, where the incense was burnt and prayers were offered by the high priest, was the golden altar, which was in the Holy place. The souls under the altar referred to here, were alive and conscious talking to the Lord and, therefore, the scene is in heaven. These souls had white robes given to them signifying that they were saved from their sins, and were righteous before God.

It also shows that the souls do not die or lose conscience or cease to exist when man dies. The souls were alive, seeking a quick avenge of their blood shed by the earth-dwellers. However, they were told that the Lord knows the appropriate time to avenge their blood and surely He does so in due season.

In Matthew 19:28 Jesus said to His disciples that in the new world, when He sits on His glorious throne, they will also sit on their twelve thrones and judge the twelve tribes of Israel. This judgment refers to "the judgment seat of Christ" where rewards are given. Daniel prophesied about this judgment.

"As I looked, thrones were placed, and the Ancient of Days took his seat; his clothing was white as snow, and the hair of his head like pure wool; his throne was fiery flames; its wheels were burning fire" Daniel 7:9

"For the Son of man shall come in the glory of his Father with his angels; and then he shall reward every man according to his works" (Matthew 16:27)

CHAPTER 19
PAUL'S BOLDNESS

Saul accepted Jesus as his Lord and after his conversion he was known as Paul. He became a great Apostle and served God. He was basically a Minister to the Gentiles of the Gospel of Jesus Christ. Saul's conversion was interesting.

Saul was persecuting the followers of Lord Jesus Christ by threatening with slaughter. He obtained letters from High Priest and while he was on his way to Damascus suddenly a light shone round about him and it was light from heaven. Saul fell to the ground and heard a voice, "Saul, Saul, why persecutest thou me?" Saul said, "Who art thou, Lord? And the Lord said, I am Jesus whom thou persecutest: it is hard for thee to kick against the pricks" (Acts 9:5)

Saul humbled himself and asked the Lord as to what the Lord wanted him to do. The Lord said to him to go to the city where He would show what he has to do. Men who accompanied heard the voice but did not see any one and they were surprised. Saul rose up from the ground and could not see any one. Those who accompanied him led him by the hand to Damascus. Ananias, a disciple of Jesus, went to Saul with great reluctance; yet obeying the instructions of the Lord and prayed for him, calling him Brother Saul. After that Saul received sight and was filled with Holy Spirit and immediately he started preaching that Jesus Christ was the Son of God.

Psalmist writes in Psalm Chapter 2:1 "Why do the heathen rage, and the people imagine a vain thing?" This was a prophecy about Lord Jesus Christ who is the Son of God.

AMID PERSECUTIONS

Paul writes: "What shall we then say to these things? If God be for us, who can be against us?" (Romans 8:31)

Who can stand against God and the children of God? It appears outwardly that people are persecuting the children of God but it is impossible to do so without touching the apple of the eye of God himself. When people persecute the servants of God, it is tantamount to touching the apple of the eye of God. Without God's knowledge no one can do anything to the child of God. People who persecute the children of God will surely reap consequences of their actions. But they children of God who face persecutions will have their rewards. Stephen knew about the heavenly rewards for him. He looked up into heaven and while giving up the spirit he cried to the Lord to forgive those who were hurting him. Jesus himself said on the cross that those who were crucifying him did not know what they were doing and, therefore, he cried to the Father to forgive them.

Saul could neither persecute any one; nor was the persecution launched against him for standing for Christ was successful. Paul faced illegal charges and was imprisoned; yet he faced and defended himself with great courage. God was with him always.

The Jews heard Saul preach in the very beginning days of his conversion that Jesus is the Son of God and Jesus is the very Christ. Unable to tolerate his preaching the Jews took counsel to kill him. This was the beginning of Paul's own persecution and for living for Christ. It is evident from Chapters 21 to 28 of the Book of Acts that Apostle Paul was by nature a very bold man and faced persecutions and accusations with great courage.

"Thrice was I beaten with rods, once was I stoned, thrice I suffered shipwreck, a night and a day I have been in the deep". 2 Corinthians 11:25

Agabus, a prophet during his days prophesied against Paul that he will be arrested by the Jews and will be given over to the Gentiles, but he never got discouraged. He was falsely alleged and was put in prison. Paul boldly defended himself. Paul faced shipwrecks but was never discouraged. He encouraged others. He wrote to Timothy, whom he considered as his son in the Lord,

"Holding faith, and a good conscience; which some having put away concerning faith have made shipwreck": (1 Timothy 1:19)

In 2 Corinthians 12th Chapter Paul wrote that he had weakness, which is not clearly revealed to us. He prayed to God three times to take away that weakness, but God said to him that in Paul's weakness was God's strength.

"And he said unto me, My grace is sufficient for thee: for my strength is made perfect in weakness. Most gladly therefore will I rather glory in my infirmities, that the power of Christ may rest upon me". (2 Corinthians 12:9)

CHAPTER 20
PAUL TURNS TO GENTILES

Acts Chapter 13 has details about Apostle Paul's endeavors to turn Jews from their obstinate stance of rejection of Jesus as their Messiah. He details great many events that have taken place in the past right from the days of Abraham until the resurrection of Jesus.

Paul tried to convey the message of salvation that is available only in Lord Jesus Christ but Jews not only stirred up the devout and honorable women and the chief men of the Antioch, but also persecuted Paul and Barnabas. They expelled them from their region. As Lord Jesus Christ commanded his disciples to shake off the dust against that city and go ahead to another city (Matthew 10:14)

Paul and Barnabas followed the example and they shook off the dust off their feet against them. The disciples were filled with joy and with the Holy Spirit.

It started when the CHURCH at Antioch had prophets and teachers among whom were four names were prominent. They were: (1) Barnabas (2) Simeon who was also called Niger (3) Lucius of Cyrene and (4) Manaen

The Holy Spirit separated Paul and Barnabas for working for Lord Jesus Christ. The Church laid hands on Paul and Barnabas and sent them for work. This was a follow up of what Lord Jesus wanted from Paul. Lord Jesus Christ called Saul and said about him that "...he is a chosen vessel unto me, to bear my name before the Gentiles, and kings, and the children of Israel" (Acts 9:15) Saul was called by the name Paul.

AMID PERSECUTIONS

This was the beginning of the ministry by Paul first to the Jews and then to the Gentiles. Earlier Peter spoke to the men of Israel (Ref. Acts Chapters 1 and 2). The early ministry of Paul and Barnabas was not an easy one. They were sent out into the midst of powerful unbelieving men of Israel and then to the Gentiles. The Church and the Ministry was in the beginning stages. As they were traveling from Selucia and from there to Cyprus they encountered many hardships.

One of the toughest encounters they faced was with a sorcerer, who was a Jew and a false prophet, whose name was Barjesus. After dealing with this sorcerer they had another sorcerer come in their way and his name was Elymas, who opposed preaching of the Gospel of Jesus Christ.

When they were at Salamis they preached the word of God in the SYNAGOGUES of the Jews. Paul and Barnabas had John also with them for working for the Lord. While they were passing through that isle to Paphos, they came across Barjesus, who was with the deputy of the country, Sergius Paulus. Sergius was a wise man and he called Paul and Barnabas and desired to hear the word of God from them. Elymas opposed preaching of the word of God to Sergius Paulus thinking that Sergius would turn away from his faith. Paul filled with the Holy Spirit set his eyes on Elymas and said to him...

"O full of all subtilty and all mischief, thou child of the devil, thou enemy of all righteousness, wilt thou not cease to pervert the right ways of the Lord? And now, behold, the hand of the Lord is upon thee, and thou shalt be blind, not seeing the sun for a season" (Acts 13:10)

Elymas lost sight "for a season" because of the curse and seeing this deputy Sergius Paulus believed in the Lord.

AMID PERSECUTIONS

From Paphos Paul, Barnabas and John went to Perga in Pemphylia. From there John departed from then and returned to Jerusalem. Paul and Barnabas departed from Perga and came to Antioth in Pisidia and went to SYNAGOGUE on the Sabbath day and sat down. The rulers of the SYNAGOGUE sent unto them to speak if they have anything to speak about the law, prophets.

Paul then stood and addressed them as "Men of Israel, and ye that fear God, give audience."

Paul went on describing in detail as to how God of the people of Israel chose the patriarchs and exalted them when they were as strangers in the land of Egypt.

With great might God delivered them from the bondage under Pharaoh. God destroyed seven nations when they were on their journey from Egypt to Canaan. God gave to them Judges to guide them in the way of the Lord for four hundred and fifty years until Samuel the prophet. But then they desired to have a king to rule over them.

God gave Saul the son of Cis, one who was of the tribe of Benjamin, for forty years. God removed him and raised up unto them David to be their king and the Lord himself said that he found David, the son of Jesse as a man after his own heart and that he will fulfill His will. God raised up from the seed of David a Savior unto Israel and his name was Jesus.

John the Baptist preached the repentance by Baptism to all the people of Israel. John said he was not worthy to lose the latchet of the One who comes after him. Paul says that the salvation was sent out to the men and brethren, children of the stock of Abraham, and whosoever fears God.

Every Sabbath day these men of Jerusalem and their rulers who read in the SYNAGOGUES the law and prophet did not yet believe on Jesus but condemned him. They found no reason to kill Jesus, yet they desired of Pilate the Jesus should be slain. When they had fulfilled everything that was written of him they took him down from the cross and laid in a sepulcher. But God raised him from the dead. Jesus was seen by many during those days and Paul says Paul and his Barnabas were witnesses to these events.

Paul tells the audience that Jesus the Messiah had come as prophesied (Psalm Chapter 2:7) and God raised him from the dead and he will have sure mercies of David. Even as David saw corruption and was laid to rest along with his fathers, no one could see corruption in Jesus. This was also in fulfillment of prophesying as prophesied. (Psalms 16:10) Paul then declares that through the Son of man was preached the forgiveness of sins. He declares that all those who believe him are justified from all things from which they could not be justified by the law of Moses.

Prophet Habakkuk had burden for the children of Israel that they were going away from the Lord and slack in following the commandments of the Lord. The prophet cries out to God showing his concern for them and says how long these people would go unpunished for their wickedness and iniquity. The Lord says that he would raise up Chaldeans against them and scatter them. God warned about this in earlier as we read in Deuteronomy 28:64-67. As per the word of God they were scattered and God says that he will do the work that they do not believe even if they were told about it. Paul quotes this verse in his speech and warns Jews about their disbelief and rejection of Jesus as their Messiah.

AMID PERSECUTIONS

Behold ye among the heathen, and regard, and wonder marvellously: for I will work a work in your days, which ye will not believe, though it be told you. (Habakkuk 1:5)

As prophesied earlier the Jews did neither accept Jesus as their Messiah nor did Apostle Paul as one sent to preach the gospel of Jesus Christ. The Gentiles came in when they saw that Jews left from the SYNAGOGUE and requested Paul and Barnabas to preach to them the same message that they spoke to the Jews the next Sabbath day.

Congregation was divided over this issue and may Jews and religious proselyte followed Paul and Barnabas. Paul and Barnabas advised all of them to continue in the grace of God. Almost the whole city came together to hear the word of God from Paul and Barnabas the next Sabbath day. But the envy in Jews grew more when they saw the multitudes following Paul and Barnabas and spoke against them and said to the multitude that Paul and Barnabas were contradicting and blaspheming.

It was then that Paul and Barnabas became bold and said that it was necessary that the word of God should have been first spoken to the Jews and admonished that they were not worthy of everlasting life. It was then that they turned to the Gentiles. It was then that Paul said that he was set apart to take the Gospel of Jesus Christ and the message of salvation to the Gentiles unto the ends of the earth.

When the Gentiles heard these words from Apostle Paul they were glad and glorified the word of the Lord and as many as were elected by God unto eternal life believed. The word of the Lord was published the entire region. When the Jews expelled them they shook off the dust off their feet and went to Iconium. (Acts 13:40-52)

CHAPTER 21
FOLLOW JESUS: NO EXCUSES

As a result of seeing miracles from Lord Jesus Christ there was a great multitude following Him, may not be much to hear message from Him, but to see they were healed of their sickness. Jesus gave commandment that they all depart to the other side of Capernaum, which was Sea of Galilee. At this time a scribe came to Him and said that he will follow Jesus wherever he went. It is quite possible that this scribe did not really want to follow but it may be that he thought of earning some finances or fame by being with the Lord. Jesus said to him that...

"The foxes have holes, and the birds of the air have nests; but the Son of man hath not where to lay his head" Matthew 8:20

Jesus was born of the Virgin Mary conceived in her of the Holy Ghost. He, who was "in the form of God, thought it not robbery to be equal with God: But made himself of no reputation, and took upon him the form of a servant, and was made in the likeness of men" (Philippians 2:6-7)

"He came unto his own, and his own received him not" (John 1:11)

It was not as easy to follow Jesus as the scribe thought it is. One of the twelve disciples betrayed Jesus and rest of them left Him when He was about to be crucified. Jesus said to them that "the sheep of the flock shall be scattered abroad" (Matt 26:31b) and as He prophesied all of them left Him on the day He was crucified. Peter denied Him three times before the cock crew the night before his crucifixion, but later he repented and proclaimed the Gospel of Jesus Christ boldly.

AMID PERSECUTIONS

There was another man, who perhaps half-heartedly, was following Jesus for reasons best known to him. Jesus asked him to follow Him but he requested permission from the Lord that he may be allowed to go and first bury his father. That was an excuse! The phrase 'to go and bury the father' is usually used to show indifference or to postpone an assigned task. Yet another said he may be permitted to go and bid farewell to those who are at his home. That was an excuse too! Jesus said to him that no one who puts his hand to the plough and looks back is fit for the kingdom of God.

"And he said unto another, Follow me. But he said, Lord, suffer me first to go and bury my father. Jesus said unto him, Let the dead bury their dead: but go thou and preach the kingdom of God. And another also said, Lord, I will follow thee; but let me first go bid them farewell, which are at home at my house. And Jesus said unto him, No man, having put his hand to the plough, and looking back, is fit for the kingdom of God". (Luke 9:59-62)

When Jesus called Peter and his brother Andrew, fishers by profession, saying "Follow me and I will make you fishers of men" they were casting a net into the sea and they did not hesitate or tell Him excuses. Similarly, when Jesus called James, the son of Zebedee and John his brother, they were helping their father in mending their nets. They too did not hesitate nor did they say any excuse. Matthew, the tax collector followed Jesus immediately when he was called. (Ref. Matthew 4:18-22, Matthew 9:9)

The cost of discipleship is huge but the rewards the disciple receives are worth counting more than any treasure on this earth. No matter a follower would face hardships or persecutions for His name sake, yet they are blessed.

"Blessed are they which are persecuted for righteousness' sake: for theirs is the kingdom of heaven. Blessed are ye, when men shall revile you, and persecute you, and shall say all manner of evil against you falsely, for my sake. Rejoice, and be exceeding glad: for great is your reward in heaven: for so persecuted they the prophets which were before you" (Matthew 5:10-12)

"Blessed are they that do his commandments, that they may have right to the tree of life, and may enter in through the gates into the city" (Revelation 22:14)

CHAPTER 22
PAUL AND PERSECUTIONS

"And I punished them oft in every synagogue, and compelled them to blaspheme; and being exceedingly mad against them, I persecuted them even unto strange cities" (Acts 26:11)

Apostle Paul testifies before King Agrippa as to how he went before his conversion to Damascus with authority and commission from chief priests to persecute Christians and the Church and says to him "At midday, O king, I saw in the way a light from heaven, above the brightness of the sun, shining round about me and them which journeyed with me. And when we were all fallen to the earth, I heard a voice speaking unto me, and saying in the Hebrew tongue, Saul, Saul, why persecutest thou me? it is hard for thee to kick against the pricks. And I said, Who art thou, Lord? And he said, I am Jesus whom thou persecutes"

Lord Jesus Christ called Apostle Paul to be a minister and witness both of those things that he has seen and to deliver him from people, and from Gentiles, unto whom he was sent with the Gospel of Jesus Christ (cf. Acts 26:11-19)

Later in his life Apostle Paul faced persecutions and God was with him. He was beaten up and persecuted at Philippi when he preached Gospel of Jesus Christ and was imprisoned. Later, the authorities let him go, but Paul demanded that sergeants must themselves come and release him because he was a Roman citizen and did no wrong.

The magistrates and sergeants feared and requested Paul to leave Philippi. Thus Paul left Philippi and went to Thessalonica via Amphipolis and Apollonia. Paul established church at Thessalonica. Silas (also called Silvanus) and Timothy (also called Timotheus) helped him in his ministry. Paul reasoned three Sabbath days in the Synagogues at Thessalonica debating with them on intriguing questions about Jesus Christ, his death, burial, resurrection, and His second coming (Ref. Acts 17:1-5)

Contrary to the beliefs of Jews at Thessalonica, Paul said he preached Christ, who was crucified, died and rose from the dead. Some of them, who believed his preaching, was a great multitude from devout Greeks and women, but Jews, who did not believe his preaching were moved with envy and with the help of some "lewd fellows of baser sort" and gathered a company and not only caused uproar in the city but also assaulted the house of one named Jason.

Interest grew in people of the land and gathered more and more to listen to Paul's preaching. Seeing that Paul is gathering much importance Jews in Thessalonica were jealous and tried to harm him.

The brethren at Thessalonica sensed the trouble caused by the obstructionists and sent Paul, Silas, and Timothy by night to Berea where Paul preached Gospel to brethren at Berea in the synagogues of Jews (Ref. Acts 17:10, 18)

The believers at Berea were more interested to learn the word of God than Thessalonians. They received the word of God with all readiness but did not just believe anything preached or taught to them without searching the scriptures daily if the preaching or teaching was according to the word of God.

There is lesson for us here that we should not take every teaching as granted without referring to the scriptures if it were

AMID PERSECUTIONS

really so. Many times it so happens that listeners or readers are misguided by false teachings by emotional preaching and teaching. Bible warns us not to be taken away by false preachers or false teachings.

Many people at Berea believed Jesus Christ, as the Son of God, as preached by Paul and among those who believed were honorable women who were Greeks, and many men.

Paul faced similar circumstances as he faced at Thessalonica when Jews from Thessalonica went to Berea and stirred up people against him. Then the brethren at Berea sent away Paul to go as it were to the sea but led him from there to Athens. Paul preferred to be alone at Athens considering the ministry that was to be carried on by Silas and Timothy at Berea.

"And then immediately the brethren sent away Paul to go as it were to the sea: but Silas and Timotheus abode there still" (Acts 17:14)

After-a-while Paul sent word for Silas and Timothy to join him in his ministry and Paul went to Corinth. When Silas and Timothy joined Paul at Corinth, he sent Timothy back to Thessalonica to comfort the believers at Thessalonica and also to bring a report as to how they were doing in the Lord.

It is evident from Paul's ministry in the first century that persecutions did not hinder the growth of the Church; but rather the Churches increased and the Gospel of Jesus Christ was preached in many parts of the world. It was then true and it is now true that whenever the church is persecuted it thrived and grew rather than diminishing. God never allows the Church to diminish or to be destroyed. It is those who persecute the Church who will, eventually, be destroyed.

SECTION II
THE CHURCH GREW STRONG

CHAPTER 23
THE ONE NEW MAN

The Gospel of Grace was preached during Acts Period and many Gentiles were saved during Acts period. The Book of Acts contains historical facts of Apostles, primarily that Apostle Peter and Apostle Paul. The Book of Acts contains the historical transition of the "Kingdom" message to the message of 'One New Man" the "CHURCH", whose head is Lord Jesus Christ with members from Jews and Gentiles.

The transition could be seen from:

1. Preaching of Gospel in Jerusalem ("And the word of God increased; and the number of the disciples multiplied in Jerusalem greatly; and a great company of the priests were obedient to the faith" Acts 6:7)

2. Preaching of Gospel in Judea and Samaria ("Then had the churches rest throughout all Judaea and Galilee and Samaria, and were edified; and walking in the fear of the Lord, and in the comfort of the Holy Ghost, were multiplied". Acts 9:31)

3. Preaching of Gospel in Tyre and Sidon (Herod was smitten by God and the Church is blessed. "But the word of God grew and multiplied". Acts 12:20-24)

4. Preaching of Gospel in Asia Minor ("And so were the churches established in the faith, and increased in number daily" Acts 16:5)

5. Preaching of Gospel in Europe ("And this was known to all the Jews and Greeks also dwelling at Ephesus; and fear fell on

them all, and the name of the Lord Jesus was magnified" Acts 19:17) and 6. Preaching the Gospel in Europe:

(a) "Be it known therefore unto you, that the salvation of God is sent unto the Gentiles, and [that] they will hear it" Acts 28:28

(b) "Preaching the kingdom of God, and teaching those things which concern the Lord Jesus Christ, with all confidence, no man forbidding him" Acts 28:31)

The Gentles saved during Acts period were not circumcised to become proselytes. In Christ circumcised and un-circumcised are all equal members of the Church. Peter, James, Mark, Paul and Barnabas were as much equal members of the Church as any other Gentile, who believed in Jesus Christ as his/her personal Savior. If it is argued that there is no Church during Acts period, then it goes to say that Peter and Paul were also not members of the "Body of Christ".

"Having abolished in his flesh the enmity, even the law of commandments contained in ordinances; for to make in himself of twain one new man, so making peace" (Ephesians 2:15)

There are two verses where we find the phrase "new man", which has different meaning than that of "one new man".

"And that ye put on the new man, which after God is created in righteousness and true holiness". (Ephesians 4:24)

"And have put on the new man, which is renewed in knowledge after the image of him that created him" (Colossians 3:10)

Those verses in Ephesians 4:24 and Colossians 3:10 point towards the one who has accepted Lord Jesus Christ as personal savior and become 'new man' having put off the old man in him. He is a new creation in Christ Jesus. God considers him as righteous and holy. He is renewed in the knowledge of God who created him.

The phrase "one new man" referred to in Ephesians 2:15 is the one body of Christ that has members from Jews and Gentiles. They are made one in Christ and there is no difference between them.

There are few conditions that need to have been fulfilled before 'one new man' came into existence.

Firstly, the condition "Having abolished in his flesh the enmity, even the law of commandments contained in ordinances" should have been fulfilled.

Secondly, the one becoming part of that "one new man" should have been cleansed of his sin through the blood of Lord Jesus Christ. That is to say the person who becomes a member of that 'one new man' should have repented of his/her sin and accepted Lord Jesus Christ as his/her personal Savior. Then, obviously the 'one new man' also can be called member of the "Church", "the body of Christ" and the "Bride of Christ".

Thirdly, the condition "to make in himself of twain" should have been fulfilled.

THE FIRST CONDITION FULFILLED

The condition was fulfilled when Jesus was crucified on the cross.

"Jesus, when he had cried again with a loud voice, yielded up the ghost". (Matthew 27:50)

The veil in the Temple was rent into two from top to bottom, opening the way from Holy to the Holies and earth did quake and rocks rent. (Matthew 27:51)

The centurion and others who were with him, watching Jesus saw the earthquake and things that have happened at that time and greatly feared and acknowledged that Jesus was the "Son of God" (Matthew 27:54)

Jesus rose from the dead on the third day (Matthew 28:6), and after forty days he ascended into heaven and will come back again in the same manner he ascended into heaven. (Acts 1:9-11)

THE SECOND CONDITION FULFILLED

Bible says we all, irrespective of whether we are Jews or Gentiles, have sinned and come short of the glory of God (Romans 3:9, 23) and the wages of sin is death but the gift of God is eternal life through Jesus Christ our Lord. (Romans 6:23)

To become partakers of God's blessing and to receive salvation one has to repent of his/her sins and accept Jesus Christ as personal savior. Bible says:

"That if thou shalt confess with thy mouth the Lord Jesus, and shalt believe in thine heart that God hath raised him from the dead, thou shalt be saved" (Romans 10:9)

"If we confess our sins, he is faithful and just to forgive us our sins, and to cleanse us from all unrighteousness". (1 John 1:9)

THE THIRD CONDITION FULFILED

Whoever has accepted Lord Jesus Christ as his personal savior, whether we be Jews or Gentiles, whether we be bond or free, have been made to drink of one spirit and for by one Spirit we are all baptized into one body. (1 Corinthians 12:13)

JESUS BECAME OUR HIGH PRIEST

"For we have not an high priest which cannot be touched with the feeling of our infirmities; but was in all points tempted like as we are, yet without sin". (Hebrews 4:15)

The barrier between Jews and Gentiles was removed. That is to say, the provision for 'one new man' was made immediately when Jesus was crucified on the cross. Now the question is when exactly the Jews and Gentiles became one. Was it after Acts 28:28 or is it when Jesus was crucified on the cross?

When the day of Pentecost was fully come as we read in Acts Chapter2 there were in Jerusalem Jews, devout men, out of every nation under heaven.

"And there were dwelling at Jerusalem Jews, devout men, out of every nation under heaven". (Acts 2:5)

Also in Acts 2:9-11 there is a mention of all those who were present from different regions.

"Parthians, and Medes, and Elamites, and the dwellers in Mesopotamia, and in Judaea, and Cappadocia, in Pontus, and Asia, Phrygia, and Pamphylia, in Egypt, and in the parts of Libya about Cyrene, and strangers of Rome, Jews and proselytes, Cretes and Arabians, we do hear them speak in our tongues the wonderful works of God". (Acts 2:9-11)

AMID PERSECUTIONS

The people present there when Peter spoke of Jesus starting from Acts 2:14 were from Judea and from those who dwell at Jerusalem. Note how the scriptures clearly distinguish those who were present in Jerusalem as from "Judea" and "all ye that dwell at Jerusalem". If only Jews were there at that time, the distinction should not have been made, but the scriptures clearly distinguish two categories of people present at the time when Peter spoke about Jesus of Nazareth.

These people, who were present there in Jerusalem during the time of Pentecost, were asked by Jesus to wait in Jerusalem, until they were empowered to speak about Him. Holy Spirit, who was the "Promise of the Father", came upon all of them. Acts 2:4 says:

"And they were all filled with the Holy Ghost, and began to speak with other tongues, as the Spirit gave them utterance".

When this news was heard abroad, multitudes came together and were confused because every man heard them speak in his own language and they all understood one another. They were all amazed and marvelled and said to each other, "...Behold, are not all these which speak Galileans? And how hear we every man in our own tongue, wherein we were born?" (Acts 2:1-8)

Paul quotes Hosea Chapter 1 and says in Romans 9:25 that those Israelites who were unfaithful to God were called "Not my people" by God. They were all Gentiles. But what about those who were not the descendants of Jacob, who were present in Jerusalem at the time when Peter spoke of Jesus?

Were there no Roman Government officials? How sure is anyone to say that those who were called "Parthians, and Medes, and Elamites, and the dwellers in Mesopotamia, and in

Judaea, and Cappadocia, in Pontus, and Asia, Phrygia, and Pamphylia, in Egypt, and in the parts of Libya about Cyrene, and strangers of Rome, Jews and proselytes, Cretes and Arabians" were also the descendants of Jacob. I Chronicles Chapter 1: 17-28 have the details of sons of Shem, Elamites, and many others.

Neither scriptures nor the history records of Flavius Josephus show that all those were descendants of Jacob. They were all Gentiles. There is no basis to say that those three thousand saved when Peter preached were only Jews or descendants of Jacob.

There are some who say without producing any evidence that they were mixed generations from Jacob's descendants and pure Gentiles and there are some who say that they were all from "House of Israel" who mixed up with Samaritans without showing where those from "House of Israel" were or are now. Some try to make up some stories even from those narrations which are mystery.

"Then they that gladly received his word were baptized: and the same day there were added unto them about three thousand souls". (Acts 2:41)

Later many more souls from Jews and Gentiles were added to the Church.

"Praising God, and having favour with all the people. And the Lord added to the church daily such as should be saved" (Acts 2:47)

PETER'S MESSAGE

When Peter spoke of Jesus of Nazareth that He was a man approved of God, he had full knowledge of Jesus, because Peter

AMID PERSECUTIONS

was a disciple of Jesus Christ. Peter knew that Mary was the earthly mother of Jesus and Joseph had purposed earlier to put her off when Joseph came to know that Mary was pregnant. Jesus was born of the Virgin Mary of the Holy Spirit (Matthew 1:20).

Later in his life Peter wrote in his 1 epistle Chapter 1 a great message honoring "God the Father of our Lord Jesus Christ, who has begotten us unto a lively hope by the resurrection of Jesus Christ from the dead to an inheritance, and undefiled, and that fades not, which is reserved for us". (1 Peter 1:3-5)

This Peter, an Apostle of Jesus Christ said in Acts 2:21-24 that whosoever shall call on the name of the Lord shall be saved. This Peter addressed the men in Israel and testified about Jesus of Nazareth that he was approved of God and did miracles and wonders and signs.

Peter said that they took Jesus, who was delivered by the determinate counsel of foreknowledge of God, and killed him and that God raised Him from the pains of death, which could not hold him Jesus ascended into heaven and seated on the right hand of the Father and will come back after all his enemies are brought to His footstool.(Acts 2:21-25, 31, Psalm 16:8-11). Peter also quoted the David and his prophecy about Jesus Christ. (Psalm 110:1)

Before Peter went to meet Cornelius, an uncircumcised Gentile, a devout man, who feared God and gave much alms, and also prayed to God always, God taught a lesson to Peter. It was when Peter was still thinking about Mosaic Law and ordinances.

Even though he was hungry he had determination not to eat that which was forbidden under Mosaic Law and Ordinances.

Jesus had already ascended into heaven by this time, and the Apostles had already begun preaching the Gospel of grace. It was not the kingdom message that they were preaching, but the Gospel of Grace.

The message was that Jesus was crucified by sinful people like me, and that he died for saving the sinner, and that he was buried and rose on the third day from the dead and after forty days ascended into heaven. Peter was the first one to preach about this fact as we read in Acts Chapter 2.

Later in Acts Chapter 9 there is narration of how Paul, who persecuted Christians, was encountered by Jesus, who said that He was the one whom Paul was persecuting. When Christians are persecuted Jesus felt that he was being persecuted.

It was this Lord Jesus Christ, the Son of God, the very God himself, who said to Peter to go to Cornelius to give him the salvation message. Before going to Cornelius, Peter saw a man named "Aeneas" sick of palsy at Lydda. Peter said to him "...Jesus Christ maketh thee whole: arise, and make thy bed. And he arose immediately" (Acts 9:34). Because of this miracle done by Peter in the name of Jesus, many turned to the Lord. Later Peter prayed and raised Tabitha (also known as Dorcas) from the dead. Many believed in the Lord.

PETER IN TANNER' HOUSE

Then Peter went to Simon, who was a tanner, and stayed with him for many days. Peter did not have any hesitation to stay in the house of the tanner for many days.

"And it came to pass, that he tarried many days in Joppa with one Simon a tanner". (Acts 9:43)

CORNELIUS'S VISION

Cornelius saw an angel of God in a vision saying to him that his prayers and his alms to people were honored by God. The angel of God said to Cornelius that he should send word for Simon Peter (the disciple of Lord Jesus Christ), who stayed in the house of one named Simon, who was a tanner. Cornelius sent two of his servants to Joppa to call for Simon Peter. (Acts 10:1-8)

TANNER

A 'tanner' is the one who deals with dead animals. **International Standard Bible Encyclopedia** describes 'Tanner' as:

Quote: "tan'-er (burseus, from bursa "a hide"): The only references to a tanner are in Ac 9:43; 10:6,32. The Jews looked upon tanning as an undesirable occupation and well they might, for at best it was accompanied with unpleasant odors and unattractive sights, if not even ceremonially unclean. We can imagine that Simon the tanner found among the disciples of Jesus a fellowship which had been denied him before.

Peter made the way still easier for Simon by choosing his house as his abode while staying in Joppa. Simon's house was by the seashore, as is true of the tanneries along the Syrian coast today, so that the foul-smelling liquors from the vats can be drawn off with the least nuisance, and so that the salt water may be easily accessible for washing the skins during the tanning process.

These tanneries are very unpretentious affairs, usually consisting of one or two small rooms and a courtyard. Within are the vats made either of stone masonry, plastered within and without, or cut out of the solid rock.

The sheep or goat skins are smeared on the flesh side with a paste of slaked lime and then folded up and allowed to stand until the hair loosens. The hair and fleshy matter are removed, the skins are plumped in lime, bated in a concoction first of dog dung and afterward in one of fermenting bran, in much the same way as in a modern tannery.

The bated skins are tanned in sumach (Arabic summak), which is the common tanning material in Syria and Palestine. After drying, the leather is blackened on one side by rubbing on a solution made by boiling vinegar with old nails or pieces of copper, and the skin is finally given a dressing of olive oil. In the more modern tanneries degras is being imported for the currying processes. For dyeing the rams' skins red (Ex 25:1-40 ff) they rub on a solution of qermes (similar to cochineal; see DYEING), dry, oil, and polish with a smooth stone" **Unquote**.

Bible emphasizes Peter's stay in the house of a tanner: When Bible mentions specifically an incidence it is not without any significance. It needs serious consideration.

"And it came to pass, that he tarried many days in Joppa with one Simon a tanner". (Acts 9:43)

"He lodgeth with one Simon a tanner, whose house is by the sea side: he shall tell thee what thou oughtest to do". (Acts 10:6)

It was one just before Peter spoke to Cornelius, who was a Roman uncircumcised Gentile from Italian Band. Cornelius was baptized later. Points to note Tanning is unclean. Tanner is unclean. Gentiles were unclean in the sight of Jews. Yet God said what he called as 'clean' man should not call it as 'unclean'.

Hebrew Strong's Number 2931 is "tame' " transliterated as "taw-may' "

In KJV the word "Unclean" is mentioned as defiled, 5; infamous, 1; polluted, 1; pollution, 1; unclean, 79

Greek Strong's number 169 transliterated as "Akathartos" is found in KJV as

KJV (30) - foul, 2; unclean, 28;

"Or if a soul touch any unclean thing, whether it be a carcase of an unclean beast, or a carcase of unclean cattle, or the carcase of unclean creeping things, and if it be hidden from him; he also shall be unclean, and guilty". Leviticus 5:2 and also there are more details about dietary restrictions imposed on the children of Israel. These instructions included that they shall eat the beasts that have

- Parted hoof
- Cloven-footed and
- Chew the cud

But they shall not

- Camel because he chews the cud, but has no divided hoof
- Coney because he chews the cud, but has no divided hoof
- Hare because he chews the cud, but has no divided hoof
- Swine because he chews the cud, but has no divided hoof

God said the children of Israel shall not eat their flesh and they shall not touch their carcasses. They are all considered as 'Unclean" by God. (Leviticus 11:2-8)

PETER'S VISION

On the morrow when the servants of Cornelius were reaching the city, Peter went upon the housetop to pray. It was about sixth hour and Peter was very hungry. Before he went to eat with Tanner, he saw a vision. In the vision he saw heaven opened and a certain vessel descending towards him. It was like a great sheet knit at the four corners and let down to the earth. The sheet contained variety of animals; four-footed beasts, wild beasts, creeping things and fowls of the air. Peter heard a voice saying to him to rise, kill and eat. But Peter refused to eat because there were animals that were prohibited to be eaten as per Mosaic Law and ordinances. Peter said that he had never eaten that which is common or unclean. The voice said to him second time, and Peter refused to eat. The voice said to Peter that what God had cleansed should not be called common by him. This was done three times and the sheet was retrieved into heaven. (Acts 10:10-16)

PETER MEETS CORNELIUS

While Peter was in trance and thought on the vision, the Spirit spoke to him and said to him that three men were seeking him. Peter was asked to arise and go with them without doubting. Peter obeyed the voice and went with the men to Cornelius and said that he was Peter. Just before Peter identified himself Cornelius fell on the feet of Peter and worshipped him; but Peter lifted him and said that he was also a man. He meant that God is the only One who is to be worshipped and none else.

AMID PERSECUTIONS

Peter saw in the home of Cornelius many others who were there to listen to him. Peter, who was a Jew, asked

Cornelius, who was an un-circumcised Gentile, as to why he sent word for him knowing fully well that it was unlawful for Jew to keep company with Gentile. Cornelius said to Peter that he saw a man in bright clothing stood before him four days ago when he was fasting and said to him that his prayers were honored and his alms were recognized by God. Cornelius continued saying that the man, whom he saw, asked him to send word for Peter, specifically mentioning the name as Simon, whose name was Peter, and who was staying with a 'tanner'. That is the reason why he called for him and said that they were all there to hear what God had to say to all of them in his house.

SALVATION TO CORNELIUS

After Peter spoke to the congregation consisting people from various nations and tongues the message of salvation as we read in Acts Chapter 2, when the Holy Spirit fell on them and they all talked in many languages that could be understood by everyone, the gospel of Jesus Christ that peter gave to Cornelius, a Gentile, was a full message of grace, whereby a person can have salvation.

Peter spoke saying with God there is no partiality and that whoever works righteous and fears God is accepted by Him. Peter said that Jesus of Nazareth is the Lord of all, and that preached peace unto the children of Israel and the baptism that John preached.

The word was published throughout Judea from Galilee. Jesus of Nazareth did miracles and healed the sick after he was

AMID PERSECUTIONS

anointed with the Holy Spirit and with power. Jesus also cast away evil spirits from those who were oppressed of the devil.

Peter testified that The Father in heaven was with Jesus, the Son of God, and that the disciples were all witnesses to the preaching, and miracles of Jesus of Nazareth. They were witnesses to all that they saw in the land of Jews, and in Jerusalem, and yet Jesus was killed and he was hung on the Cross.

God raised Jesus the third day and He appeared to all of them on different occasions and ate and drank with them. Peter said that Jesus asked them to preach to people that He was ordained of God to be the Judge of the quick and the dead. All the prophets spoke about Jesus and whoever believes in Him shall receive remission of sins. While Peter was still speaking Holy Spirit fell on all of them that heard the Gospel of Jesus Christ.

The Jews, and the brethren, who came with Peter, were surprised to see that Holy Spirit fell on all of them to whom Gospel of Jesus Christ was preached. They all spoke in tongues and magnified God. Then Peter asked if there is any obstruction for them to be baptized in the name of the Lord and commanded them to be baptized in the name of the Lord. They requested Peter to stay with them for few more days. (Acts 10:19-48)

Apostles and brethren, who were in Judea, heard that Gentiles also received the word of God and they spoke in tongues. When Peter went to Jerusalem they argued with him as to why he went to Gentiles and ate with them. Their questioning was based on the instructions of Jesus who earlier said to them that they should not go in the way of Gentiles.

"These twelve Jesus sent forth, and commanded them, saying, Go not into the way of the Gentiles, and into any city of the Samaritans enter ye not" (Matthew 10:5)

Peter recollects this after Cornelius receives salvation that God was teaching him a lesson that whether it be Jew or Gentile, circumcised or un-circumcised, everyone who receives salvation is equal in the sight of God and none is 'common' or 'unclean'.

Peter rehearsed before them the entire vision when he saw 'common' and 'unclean' animals in a vessel on a sheet that descended from heaven and a voice asked him to rise, kill and eat them; and that he refused. But the voice said to him that he should not call as 'common" and "unclean" that which God has cleansed (Acts 11:1-10).

CORNELIUS BECOMES MEMBER OF THE CHURCH

Cornelius became a member of "THE CHURCH".

Salvation to Gentiles was already in the plan of God. Israel is blinded in order that Gentiles may receive salvation. (Romans 11:6-8, 2 Corinthians 3:14)

Isaiah's prophecy was fulfilled by Jesus.

"That it might be fulfilled which was spoken by Esaias the prophet, saying, Behold my servant, whom I have chosen; my beloved, in whom my soul is well pleased: I will put my spirit upon him, and he shall shew judgment to the Gentiles. He shall not strive, nor cry; neither shall any man hear his voice in the streets. A bruised reed shall he not break, and smoking flax shall he not quench, till he send forth judgment unto victory. And in his name shall the Gentiles trust". (Matthew 12:17-21, Cf. Isaiah 42:3)

Abraham, who was the father of faith, was the root of Olive Tree. Gentiles, who are compared to wild Olive Tree, believed in Jesus as their savior, the unbelieving Jews were cut off and believing Gentiles were grafted into the Natural Olive Tree in their places and thereby Jews and Gentiles are made one in Christ. They became the body of Christ, and they are all collectively called the "bride" of Christ'. The Gentiles who believed Jesus as their savior were saved by grace through their faith in Jesus and became partakers of the root who is Abraham, who was known as father of faith. Both Abraham's descendants through Isaac, and Jacob, the believing Jews, along with unbelieving Gentiles are now the members the 'Church", whose head is Lord Jesus Christ, who identified himself as the true "vine".

"And if some of the branches be broken off, and thou, being a wild olive tree, wert graffed in among them, and with them partakest of the root and fatness of the olive tree" (Romans 11:17)

Apostle Paul's analogy of wild olive branches being grafted into natural olive tree is to mean that the Gentiles are made equal partners in the spiritual blessings along with Jews. Some of the natural branches were cut off because of their unbelief and in their place the wild olive branches are grafted.

This is also not to mean that to accommodate Gentiles in the natural olive tree the branches of the natural branches were cut off, but because of their unbelief that the Jews, who are considered as natural olive branches, were cut off.

AMID PERSECUTIONS

The wild olive branches are asked not to take pride in themselves because they were grafted into natural olive tree. Paul warns that if natural branches were cut off because of their unbelief, God will not hesitate to cut off wild olive branches. This does not mean that salvation will be lost by any believer in Christ, but it only means that they will be cut off to make way for the natural branches.

Paul argues if God had cast away the natural branches and says "God forbid".

"I say then, Hath God cast away his people? God forbid. For I also am an Israelite, of the seed of Abraham, of the tribe of Benjamin" (Romans 11:1)".

Here neither Peter nor Paul said that the Gentiles who believed in Jesus and were saved by grace through faith in Him became Jews first and then had the salvation, but the argument is that by faith in Jesus Christ Jews and Gentiles became one in Christ and Gentiles have become partakers of the faith of Abraham. There is no difference whether it is Jews or Gentiles; they are all one in Christ right from the period in Acts Chapter2 when three thousand were added to the Church, and Acts Chapter 10, where we see about salvation that was granted to an uncircumcised Gentile, Cornelius as also to others who were with him, and now and even until Jesus comes again to take his bride away.

"Then they that gladly received his word were baptized: and the same day there were added unto them about three thousand souls". (Acts 2:41)

"While Peter yet spake these words, the Holy Ghost fell on all them which heard the word. And they of the circumcision which believed were astonished, as many as came with Peter, because that on the Gentiles also was poured out the gift of the Holy Ghost. For they heard them speak with tongues, and magnify God. Then answered Peter" (Acts 10:44-46)

The Church came into existence in Acts Chapter2 and the "One New Man" is the Church, which has members from Jewish community and from Gentiles. They are all one in Christ.

"So we, being many, are one body in Christ, and every one members one of another" (Romans 12:5)

There is neither Jew nor Greek, there is neither bond nor free, there is neither male nor female: for ye are all one in Christ Jesus. (Galatians 3:28)

SECTION III
THE FUTURE

CHAPTER 24
FOR HIS HOLY NAME SAKE PART I

From Ezekiel 36:1-15

PROPHECY TO THE MOUTAINS OF ISRAEL

God said to Ezekiel the prophet to prophesy to the mountains of Israel. Yes to the mountains that were desolate that they should hear the word of the LORD.

It begins with the phrase, as usually, with the prefix "Thus says the LORD God", which is to mean that the words that the prophet speaks are not from the prophet but are of the LORD God. Prophet is an instrument used by the LORD to convey His message. The LORD is Jehovah, who is the only God, the God of heavens and the earth, who lives forever and ever.

Israel never had a glowing history of being obedient to the LORD, but their history is filled with failures and disobedience to the LORD. It is not because the children of Israel deserved to be brought back to their land that the LORD brought them back but because He made promises to Abraham, the father of nations and Israel, reiterated to his son Isaac, and to his grandson Jacob that the promised child is Isaac, whose lineage continued through David and Lord Jesus Christ.

The LORD chastised the children of Israel whenever they disobeyed Him, but He did not leave them like orphans. The chastisement for their disobedience was very serious and the nations thought the children of Israel will never be restored to their former condition. They made fun of them and their land. When the LORD withdrew His grace from them the nations took possession of their land. When they called curse upon themselves for crucifying Jesus they had it in full. Their land became desolate and they were scattered all over the world. However, the LORD brought them back to their land and restored their language Hebrew as national language again.

Israel's history shows that they did not keep the LORD's commandments and statutes. He said to David and to his son Solomon that if they kept the commandment of the LORD they will have peace and will be blessed. God also promised that if they kept His statutes there shall be continually a king on the throne of David, but Solomon failed miserably and his kingdom became a bygone word. However, when they repented of their sins the LORD had compassion on them. (cf. Deuteronomy 28:37, Jeremiah 24:9)

"O Lord, according to all thy righteousness, I beseech thee, let thine anger and thy fury be turned away from thy city Jerusalem, thy holy mountain: because for our sins, and for the iniquities of our fathers, Jerusalem and thy people are become a reproach to all that are about us". (Daniel 9:16)

The nations saw their pathetic condition and they mocked at them. The LORD was not pleased with such mockery that His children suffered at the hands of nations. They said "Aha! And took pride in saying that "The ancient heights have become our possession".

In order to humble the nations who took pride in the pathetic condition of the children of Israel, and because they thought they had victory over Israel with their might and wisdom, the LORD says to the mountains to hear His word.

It is precisely because the nations made the land of Israel desolate and crushed the children of Israel from all sides the LORD says, therefore, "O mountains of Israel, hear the word of the LORD God". The children of Israel became the cause for gossip of the people. They became the possession of the nations as a result of God's anger over them.

No one is appointed as judges to judge Israel for their failures to obey the LORD. The LORD alone is the God who chastises them and restores them for His holy name sake. It is not because they deserved to be restored as a nation that they were brought back to their land but because it is for His Holy Name sake that the LORD restored them as a nation in 1948. God takes care of them.

When the heathen nations mocked at the children of Israel God turned against and punished them for mocking. He will do it again in the future also. The "mountains and the hills, the ravines and the valleys, the desolate wastes and the deserted cities" of Israel became a prey and derision to the rest of the nations all around, because the LORD chastised them for their sins.

The LORD God says, "Surely I have spoken in my hot jealousy against the rest of the nations and against all Edom, who gave my land to themselves as a possession with wholehearted joy and utter contempt, that they might make its pasturelands a prey", which was reference to Nebuchadnezzar who with his determination came against Jerusalem and took possession of it.

In the book of Hosea we see how God said about the children of Israel that He will not have mercy on them, and He will not be their God, and called them "empty vine", and yet because He made promises to Abraham, Isaac, and Jacob, He said to them later that they are His people, and He will have mercy on them.

Therefore, the LORD says to Ezekiel to prophecy concerning the land of Israel, and say to the mountains, to the hills, to the rivers, and to the valleys that the LORD spoke in His jealousy and in His fury because they bore shame of the heathen for a season, but the nations, who persecuted them, will suffer reproach perpetually.

According to the LORD's prophecy the mountains of Israel shall shoot forth their branches and yield their fruit to the LORD's people Israel. The children of Israel will come home soon. The LORD assures the mountains that He is for them and He will turn to them. They will be tilled and sown, and the LORD will multiply all the people of house of Israel. The cities will be inhabited and waste places will be rebuilt.

The LORD will multiply men and animals, who in turn shall multiply and be fruitful. The LORD will restore them as in their time past, and will love them even greater than ever before. Then they will know that He is the LORD. The LORD not only lets His people walk in their cities, but He will bring forth life and happiness again for other people also to walk in their cities and mountains.

The children of Israel shall possess the land and the mountains, and the land and the mountains will be their inheritance. The LORD will not allow Israel to be deprived of their children. The LORD says because the nations say to them that they devour people and they bereave their nation of children, therefore, they shall no longer devour people and no longer bereave their nation of children. It is a declaration of the LORD. The LORD will not allow them to hear anymore the reproach of the nations.

They will no longer bear the disgrace of the peoples and no longer cause their nations to stumble. It is the declaration of the LORD.

God says when someone does some harm to you, seek the help of God and He takes pity on your helpless condition and intervenes on your behalf. He gives you strength to deal with the situation and the LORD avenges your insult on your enemy because God said "Vengeance is mine".

"Dearly beloved, avenge not yourselves, but rather give place unto wrath: for it is written, Vengeance is mine; I will repay, saith the Lord" (Romans 12:19)

CHAPTER 25
FOR HIS HOLY NAME PART II

(FROM EZEKIEL 36:16-38)

The word of the LORD came to Ezekiel the prophet calling him as "Son of man", and explained to him as to how the "House of Israel", (Northern Kingdom of Israel), defiled the land by their ways and deeds that included idolatry introduced by the tribes of Dan, Ephraim, and Kings Jeroboam, Ahab and his wife Jezebel etc. None of the nineteen kings, who ruled the northern kingdom of Israel, did what was right in the sight of the LORD.

The LORD likened their idolatry and their abominations to the uncleanness of a woman in her menstrual impurity. They shed blood upon the land with their sacrifices to the idols and polluted the land causing the LORD to pour out His fury upon them, and scattering them among the nations. The LORD judged them according to their ways and their deeds and scattered them in many countries in the world. No one ever thought that their land which became desolate, and their language which became extinct, would ever be revived. The prophecies in Ezekiel Chapters 36 and 37 were fulfilled to the letter, and they became a nation in 1948 A.D. and their language Hebrew became their national language once again.

Even as they wandered in the countries on the face of the earth, they profaned the LORD's holy name in that the people said of them "These are the people of the LORD, and yet they had to go out of his land."

"I said, I would scatter them into corners, I would make the remembrance of them to cease from among men: Were it not that I feared the wrath of the enemy, lest their adversaries should behave themselves strangely, and lest they should say, Our hand is high, and the LORD hath not done all this" (Deuteronomy 32:26-27)

Amid all such profanity the "House of Israel" brought to the LORD among the nations the LORD's concern was for His Holy Name which they were defiling. If only He was not concerned of His holy name, perhaps their restoration would have been a remote possibility.

Incorrigible as they were, the children of Israel defiled the name of the LORD wherever they went, but the LORD had concern for His holy name, and the promises that He made to their fathers, Abraham, Isaac, and Jacob. It is that immense concern of the LORD of His Holy name that compelled Him to have mercy on them and call them as His people over and over again.

"I am the LORD: that is my name: and my glory will I not give to another, neither my praise to graven images" (Isaiah 42:8)

THE LORD PUTS HIS SPIRIT WITHIN THEM

In view of the fact that they continually defiled the name of the LORD and deserved repeated chastisement, whereby the heathen nations derided of their pathetic condition, as if the LORD was not capable of helping them, the only alternative for the LORD was to put His spirit within them and give them a soft and yielding heart to obey the LORD and be obedient to Him.

The LORD commands Ezekiel the prophet to say to the "house of Israel" that it was not for their sake that the LORD was about to unite them with the "house of Judah" (the southern kingdom of Israel), but for the sake of the concern He had for His holy

name, which they profaned among the nations wherever they went.

The LORD says He will vindicate before the eyes of the nations, the holiness of His great name, whereby the nations will know that He is the LORD. He promises that He will take them out of the nations and gather them from all countries, and bring them into their own land. He says He will sprinkle as much clean water on them as to cleanse them of their un-cleanness caused by their idolatry.

The LORD says He will remove their stony heart, the stubborn heart and will give them a new heart of flesh, and will put within them a new Spirit that will make them to walk in His ways and obedient to His statutes.

This alludes to the stony places where some of the seeds fell upon stony places and did not spring up because there was no depth of the earth and the Lord explains the parable saying the man with stony heart receives the word of God but when tribulation or persecution comes along he is offended. (cf. Matthew 13:5, 20-21)

The LORD promises them that there will no more be famine in their land; instead He will fill their land with grain and fruit. He blesses their fields to produce in abundance, and will not allow their enemies to scoff at them any more. The LORD promised and reiterated that He will give them one heart and new Spirit.

"I will give them one heart and one way, that they may fear me forever, for their own good and the good of their children after them" (Jeremiah 32:39 ESV)

"And I will give them one heart, and a new spirit I will put within them. I will remove the heart of stone from their flesh and give them a heart of flesh, that they may walk in my statutes and keep my rules and obey them. And they shall be my people, and I will be their God" (Ezekiel 11:19-20 ESV)

In the New Testament similar pattern emerged in Christian Church when in the first century the multitudes, who believed, were of one heart and of one accord. They did not take pride in saying their possessions as theirs, but considered of belonging to all the believers, and gave them to the Lord.

"And the multitude of them that believed were of one heart and of one soul: neither said any of them that ought of the things which he possessed was his own; but they had all things common" (Acts 4:32)

The LORD says when He gives the "House of Israel", one heart to be in one accord, and puts a new Spirit in their hearts, it is then that they will remember their evil ways, and realize that their deeds were not good. The LORD says it is not for their sakes that He does so, but He does it for His holy name sake. He warns them to be ashamed of what they did in the past, and to loathe of their past days when they lived in sin and repent. He says that they should acknowledge over and over that He was restoring them back to their past blessed status not because they deserved it but for the LORD's holy name sake.

The blessings that the LORD will shower on them will include the cleansing of their sin and their abomination leading to their idolatry. Their land, which was desolate, will be blessed to become like the Garden of Eden, and their waste lands, and their ruined cities, will be fortified and inhabited. Consequently, the LORD will be honored, and the nations around them will see and understand that He is the LORD God, who rebuilt their ruined places, and replanted that which was desolate. The LORD says He spoke and, therefore, He will do it.

"For this is the covenant that I will make with the house of Israel after those days, declares the LORD: I will put my law within them, and I will write it on their hearts. And I will be their God, and they shall be my people" (Jeremiah 31:33)

Many times Christian Churches take the promise in Jeremiah and apply it to themselves. True Lord Jesus Christ said "… this is my blood of the new testament, which is shed for many for the remission of sins" (Matthew 26:28), but the promise that is in Jeremiah 31:33 specifically belongs to the "house of Israel" whom the LORD restores.

"This is the covenant that I will make with them after those days, saith the Lord, I will put my laws into their hearts, and in their minds will I write them" (Hebrews 10:16)

The LORD also says that He will make the "House of Israel" ask of Him to increase their people like a flock, like flock for sacrifices, like flock at Jerusalem when they celebrate the feasts of the LORD. The cities will be filled with flocks of people, and the LORD says that the people will know that He is the LORD God, the God of heavens, who lives forever and ever.

"Neither is there salvation in any other: for there is none other name under heaven given among men, whereby we must be saved" (Acts 4:12)

Salvation is in none other than Lord Jesus Christ, the Son of God, who came into this world to save sinners. Anyone responding to His call and repents of one's sin will be saved and will receive everlasting life. It is not that we loved Him first, but He loved us first and it is because He does it for His glory. When a sinner repents and is saved heaven rejoices.

"Just so, I tell you, there is joy before the angels of God over one sinner who repents." (Luke 15:10 ESV)

CHAPTER 26
DRY BONES VISION

FROM EZEKIEL CHAPER 37:1-14

The reason why it is imperative on us to worship the LORD God in spirit and in truth is because He is the creator and we are His creation. The Living God created man out of dust and breathed His Spirit into his nostrils whereby man became a living soul.

No created being could bring a new life into existence without God's intervention. Man's role in procreation is limited to his pleasure and the resultant product is the gift from God. Life in a man is the gift of God and the LORD is the owner of life.

It is quite clear from that God can shut off woman's womb or make it fruitful. Man's actions in procreation are of no use unless God intervenes and infuses life. The LORD can make the created being intelligent or fool. He can make the baby born with all limbs or no limbs. He can make a baby born blind and He can give sight to the blind.

God puts an end to life, naturally, according to His plan and desire. Man has nothing to do in what God does according to His purposes. Man is created for His glory and therefore, it is imperative that man realizes this fact and worship Him and not the creation.

Man's effort to end life is suicide and God's way of putting an end life of a believer to give him a glorified body to be with Him forever and ever. He does it according to His pleasure and in His time. Believers in Lord Jesus Christ will be conformed to His image and will see Him face to face when He comes again.

"See now that I, even I, am he, and there is no god with me: I kill, and I make alive; I wound, and I heal: neither is there any that can deliver out of my hand" (Deuteronomy 32:39)

The people of Israel, the chosen ones of the Living God prospered when they obeyed the LORD and they were chastised by the LORD when they disobeyed them. For centuries they were scattered among the nations for their disobedience to Him, and yet God being compassionate brought them back to their land and made their language Hebrew, which appeared as if it was extinct, their national language once again.

Marvelous are His ways and He did it in His own way. He gave Ezekiel vision of the marvelous work He was going to do in the lives of the children of Israel and He did it.

Ezekiel chapter 37 presents to us a very interesting prophecy, which comes immediately after the prophecy in chapter 36 and is fulfilled literally in 1948 A.D. If we look at our present status in the history of mankind it is just the chapter after Chapter 37 and before the next chapter i.e. Chapter 38. The unification of the "House of Israel" and the House of Judah is done by the LORD in a very unique and marvelous way.

The "House of Israel" was scattered among the nations for their disobedience of God's commandments and His statutes, and the "House of Judah" followed quickly the suit and God chastised them as well, when King Nebuchadnezzar of Babylon took them as captives. Their captivity lasted for seventy years and most of them returned to Jerusalem in three phases and rebuilt their temple during the days of Nehemiah, and Ezra, under the edicts of Cyrus and Artexerxes. However, many preferred to stay in Persian land.

The kingdom was not yet restored when Lord Jesus came into this world in His incarnation to save mankind from their sin. He was Jewish Messiah, who came to seek the lost and preached to them that the kingdom of heaven was at heaven, but His people for whom He came rejected Him as their Messiah and crucified Him. They called upon themselves the blood of Lord Jesus while crucifying Him, and as they desired their wish was fulfilled when Roman Emperor Titus destroyed Jerusalem in A.D 70 and killed huge number of Jews in addition to levelling Jerusalem to the ground.

The prophecy in Ezekiel Chapter 37 relates to the unification of the "House of Israel" and "House of Judah" in 1948 A.D., and the birth of a new Independent nation called "Israel" with their language Hebrew restored as their national language.

HIS MARVELOUS WORKS

Ezekiel the prophet says the hand of the LORD was upon him and the LORD brought him out in the Spirit of the LORD and set him down in the middle of the valley, which was full of bones. The LORD led him around among the bones and said to him to observe them very carefully. The bones were all very dry and too many on the surface of the valley.

The LORD asked Ezekiel a very straightforward question as to whether those bones can live or not. Ezekiel answered the LORD "O Lord GOD, you know". This response was similar to the reply Peter gave to Lord Jesus in John Chapter 21:15-19, when the Lord asked him if he loved the LORD, and it is also similar to the answer John gave to one of the twenty four elders in Revelation 7:13-14. Instead of explaining what they knew, because they either knew very little, or did not know, they preferred to say "you know".

Then the LORD said to Ezekiel to prophesy over those bones and say to them, "O dry bones, hear the word of the LORD". It was a clear call to the dead bones to hear the word of the LORD. The dead bones hear the word of the LORD not by their ability to hear or wisdom to hear but they hear because of the ability God gives them.

When a man is in sin he is like a dead bone in this world unable to respond to the word of God because his capability to respond is dead; in other words he is totally depraved. Yet, by the grace of God when the LORD wishes that they should respond, they respond to the word of the LORD.

The dry bones in the valley respond to the call of the LORD by the power the LORD God gave them. The LORD says to dry bones that He will cause breath to enter into them whereby they shall live; He will lay sinews upon them, and cause flesh to come upon them and cover them with skin, and put breath in them, whereby they live, and by such miraculous action they will know that He is the LORD.

Ezekiel prophesied as the LORD commanded him to do and as he prophesied there was a sound and "behold, a rattling, and the bones came together, bone to its bone". The prophet saw the LORD had laid sinews on them and flesh had come on them and skin covered them, yet there was no life in them. Then the LORD said to him to prophesy to the breath and say to the breath "Thus says the Lord GOD: Come from the four winds, O breath, and breathe on these slain, that they may live." As the LORD commanded him to do he prophesied and the breath came into them, and the bones lived and stood on their feet which were like an exceeding great army.

The LORD said to prophet Ezekiel that those bones were the whole house of Israel. Notice the phrase "the whole house of Israel". In human wisdom it is impossible to see that "the whole house of Israel" which is scattered all over the word beyond any one's capability of recognizing their identity, here is the LORD saying that those bones were "the whole house of Israel".

How could we not think that God is God of wonders and miracles? He made it possible for all the bones of "the whole house of Israel" to be brought into that valley. If raven could bring food and water for Elijah the prophet, then is it impossible for the LORD to order them or any other fowls or some creatures under the earth to gather the bones of "the whole house of Israel". The LORD says:

"Behold, I am the LORD, the God of all flesh. Is anything too hard for me?" Jeremiah 32:27 ESV)

The LORD says to the prophet to behold, the bones of the "House of Israel" say 'Our bones are dried up, and our hope is lost; we are indeed cut off.' What a hopeless condition they feel. Their forefathers in their hay days enjoyed the fruit of the land, which was a land with milk and honey flowing. They disobeyed the LORD and worshipped the idols, and that is the reason why they were scattered.

Now, according to the mercy of the LORD their bones are gathered in the valley and yet they seem to be hopeless. The LORD calls them "O my people" and says to them that He will open up their graves and raise them from their graves and will bring them into the land of Israel and then they will know that He is the LORD. He promises them that He will place them in their own land and put His Spirit within them and then they shall live. The LORD declares that they will know that He has spoken and that He will do it.

There is much assurance in the verses next in this chapter and we see that this prophecy is fulfilled.

SECTION IV
YIELD TO THE CREATOR

CHAPTER 27
HE IS THE CREATOR

"All things were made through him, and without him was not any thing made that was made. In him was life, and the life was the light of men. The light shines in the darkness, and the darkness has not overcome it" (John 1:3-5 ESV)

From John 1:1-2 and Philippians 2:6-7 it is clear that Jesus was with the Father partaking the divine glory and He came down into this world in the form of servant in the likeness of man relinquishing the glory that He had with the Father. John continues to write that all things were made through Him and without Him was nothing made. He is the creator of everything and in Him is the life, and the life is the light of men. The light shines in the darkness and the darkness has not overcome it.

Answering a question from Thomas Jesus said to him "I am the way, and the truth, and the life. No one comes to the Father except through me. If you had known me, you would have known my Father also. From now on you do know him and have seen him." (John 14:6-7 ESV)

God brought into existence everything from nothing by His word and He was capable of creating everything in perfection. Whatever He created, it was as it was created was perfect, and as He said it was "good" All that came into existence was, as he said in His own words, it was "good". There was no light and when the LORD said "Let there be light" there was light, and If His word is true, then there should be hypothetical questions raised as to how it came about. God's word is absolutely true and it contains truth and nothing else but the truth. His word is inerrant.

The earth was without form and void when it was created and it was as it was that is "without form and void", created as such for man to live upon it, and was perfect in the sight of the LORD. Any proposition that Satan has upset God's creation is an assumption casting aspersions on the ability of God and undermining the authority of God.

Satan was thrown out from before the presence of the LORD God and his eminence as the chief of angels was lost instantly. Satan in his fallen status could do nothing to upset God's creation. If he had the capability upset God's creation, after he fell from his eminence, as the chief of the angelic host created by God, then he would have fought to stay, in his position before he was thrown out. There is no such statement made in the scriptures that Satan had upset God's creation; nor is there a verse to show that God intended to create a huge mass of ice cube as an earth for man to ski upon.

There was no light upon the face of the earth before it was created and when it was created God saw that the light was good and the darkness could not overcome it. God separated the light from the darkness and He called the light "Day" and the darkness as "Night". Light and darkness can never live together. When the light shines the darkness is gone, and if the light is turned off the darkness appears. God did not create darkness but the darkness was on the face of the earth in the beginning.

One of the ten plagues that God inflicted in the land of Egypt was darkness when Moses, His servant, stretched out his hand, according to the command from the LORD, toward the heaven that there may be darkness upon the land of Egypt and the intensity of which could be severely felt.

AMID PERSECUTIONS

"And the LORD said unto Moses, Stretch out thine hand toward heaven, that there may be darkness over the land of Egypt, even darkness which may be felt" (Exodus 10:21)

Darkness was a plague and it was brought upon Egypt as punishment by God upon Pharaoh and his people in order that Pharaoh may repent and release the children of Israel from the bondage of slavery. Pharaoh consented to release the children of Israel from the bondage of slavery; however, when God restored light Pharaoh went back on his word, and refused to release the children of Israel. This refusal lasted until God inflicted upon them the severest plague, which was tenth in series of plagues that came upon them. God slew every first born of the Egyptians in the land of Egypt and Pharaoh had no choice than to finally bring his arrogance to the foot of the LORD, and let the children of Israel go. Nevertheless, Pharaoh pursued them again until he and his forces perished in the Red Sea.

Darkness signifies sin, rebellion the attributes of Satan. When the light came into existence the darkness disappeared. This darkness had no power over Lord Jesus Christ, who is the light of the world. He came into this world to save sinners. He is the redeemer – redeemer from sin, redeemer from darkness and redeemer from sickness. He offered Himself as a "Lamb of God" to be crucified on the cross taking upon Him our sin and die on behalf of us. He was buried and God raised Him from the dead on the third day.

"The next day John seeth Jesus coming unto him, and saith, Behold the Lamb of God, which taketh away the sin of the world" (John 1:29)

AMID PERSECUTIONS

Lord Jesus Christ lived, with his resurrected body, on this earth for forty more days after His resurrection, and many saw Him and bore witness of His resurrection. Mary Magdalene and the other Mary were at the tomb on the third day after crucifixion of Jesus but the angel said to them that Lord Jesus Christ was *not* in the tomb any more; but He rose from the dead. Jesus, after staying for forty days on this earth, ascended into heaven. The Father sent Holy Spirit into this world to comfort us, guide us and lead us in His ways.

"But the Comforter, which is the Holy Ghost, whom the Father will send in my name, he shall teach you all things, and bring all things to your remembrance, whatsoever I have said unto you" (John 14:26)

The Law was given by God through Moses to the children of Israel, but the grace and the truth came from Lord Jesus Christ. Law could not redeem anyone from sin but only pointed their transgression of the law. Their daily sacrifices were a cover for their sin but it was through Lord Jesus Christ that salvation came to all those who believed in Him.

"For the law was given by Moses, but grace and truth came by Jesus Christ" (John 1:17)

Lord Jesus Christ is the true light and He gives light to everyone, not only in this generation, but also in eternity. He, who does not have any hope, or is ignorant of his future life, after his death may know that there is life after death, and if he accepts Jesus as his personal savior, he conformed to the image of Lord Jesus Christ, when the Lord comes again. It is imperative that one needs to confess one's sins to the Lord to receive salvation. No one was saved either in the past, or will be saved in the present or in the future except by believing in Jesus as Lord and

God raised Him from the dead. He is the light of the world and in Him there is salvation.

"For God so loved the world, that he gave his only begotten Son, that whosoever believeth in him should not perish, but have everlasting life" (John 3:16)

The world that was made through Lord Jesus Christ did not know that He was the Son of God. He came to His own people, the children of Israel, and they did not receive Him. He gave the right to become the children of God, not born of fleshly body and blood, but of the will of God.

"And God said, "Let there be light," and there was light. And God saw that the light was good. And God separated the light from the darkness. God called the light Day, and the darkness he called Night. And there was evening and there was morning, the first day" (Genesis 1:2-5)

"The true light, which gives light to everyone, was coming into the world. He was in the world, and the world was made through him, yet the world did not know him. He came to his own, and his own people did not receive him. But to all who did receive him, who believed in his name, he gave the right to become children of God, who were born, not of blood nor of the will of the flesh nor of the will of man, but of God" (John 1:9-13)

CHAPTER 28
IN THE BEGINNING

(FROM JOHN 1:1-14)

"In the beginning was the Word, and the Word was with God, and the Word was God" (John 1:1)

The expression "In the beginning" was first used in Genesis 1:1. In the words of John the "Word" here points to "God" mentioned in Genesis 1:1. The LORD was before the creation. He created heavens and the earth and all that is therein. The "Word" was in existence before the creation. This is not about the man Jesus; but it is about that which became the man, the incarnate God in Jesus, as John writes in John 1:14. It reads...

"And the Word was made flesh, and dwelt among us, (and we beheld his glory, the glory as of the only begotten of the Father,) full of grace and truth" (John 1:14)

Obviously, it means Jesus is not a creature or created being but the "Word" was before the mountains were brought forth, or ever the earth and the world were created.

Psalmist says...

"Before the mountains were brought forth, or ever thou hadst formed the earth and the world, even from everlasting to everlasting, thou art God" (Psalms 90:2)

"Jesus said unto them, Verily, verily, I say unto you, Before Abraham was, I am" (John 8:58)

AMID PERSECUTIONS

More references as to who Jesus was are found in John 17:5; 6:62; 3:13; 6:46; 8:14; 16:28. Jesus is the "Son of God" who is the "Word" because He is the One through Him the Father communicated to us and promulgated His will and issued commandments.

The "Word" was with God and the "Word" was God. It implies the intimacy of the Son of God with the Father, and His divinity. He was the partaker of the divine glory. No man has seen God at any time. The only begotten Son of the Father was in the bosom of the Father and He declared unto us the Truth (cf. Hebrews 1:

"No man hath seen God at any time; the only begotten Son, which is in the bosom of the Father, he hath declared him" (John 1:18)

"God, who at sundry times and in divers manners spake in time past unto the fathers by the prophets, Hath in these last days spoken unto us by his Son, whom he hath appointed heir of all things, by whom also he made the worlds; Who being the brightness of his glory, and the express image of his person, and upholding all things by the word of his power, when he had by himself purged our sins, sat down on the right hand of the Majesty on high" (Hebrews 1:1-3)

John makes it clear that no man has ascended up to heaven, but only Lord Jesus Christ who came down from heaven, who was in heaven has ascended up to heaven.

And no man hath ascended up to heaven, but he that came down from heaven, even the Son of man which is in heaven. (John 3:13)

Apostle Paul makes it much clear to us.

"Who, being in the form of God, thought it not robbery to be equal with God: But made himself of no reputation, and took upon him the form of a servant, and was made in the likeness of men: And being found in fashion as a man, he humbled himself, and became obedient unto death, even the death of the cross. Wherefore God also hath highly exalted him, and given him a name which is above every name: That at the name of Jesus every knee should bow, of things in heaven, and things in earth, and things under the earth" (Philippians 2:6-10)

The Gospels of Matthew, Mark and Luke are called "Synoptic Gospels". According to Webster's dictionary Synopsis means a general view. The Gospel of John stands out as unique in presenting Jesus as the Son of God. John concludes his Gospel by writing that he did not write all that Jesus did inasmuch as they were too many to be recorded (John 20:30-31; John 21:25). The emphasis John lays is on the fact that Jesus is the Christ, the Son of God and that by believing this fact we may have life through His name.

The Gospel of Matthew emphasizes on the lineage of Lord Jesus Christ that He is from Abraham and through David, and that He is the Messiah about whom Old Testament prophets spoke. (cf. Matthew 1:17). The Gospel of Mark emphasizes that Jesus is the servant (Mark 1:9). The Gospel of Luke emphasizes that Jesus is the perfect one tracing back his lineage up to Adam (Luke 3:23-38)

John's Gospel is considered as the best book with respect to evangelism. The first few verses from Chapter 1 of John's Gospel speak of fundamentals. Speaking of Jesus Isaiah the prophet writes:

"For unto us a child is born, unto us a son is given: and the government shall be upon his shoulder: and his name shall be called Wonderful, Counsellor, The mighty God, The everlasting Father, The Prince of Peace" (Isaiah 9:6)

John 1:6 records about John the Baptist who was forerunner of Lord Jesus Christ and he prepared the way before Him (cf. Malachi 3:1; Matthew 11:10; Mark 1:2; Luke 1:76, and Isiah 40:3-5)

Jesus is the mediator of the covenant.

And to Jesus the mediator of the new covenant, and to the blood of sprinkling, that speaketh better things than that of Abel. (Hebrews 12:24)

Jews earnestly desired to see Messiah, their long prophesied Savior. However, when Jesus came they refused Him as the Messiah and crucified Him. The Samaritan woman knew that Messiah would come and she said "when he is come, he will tell us all things" (cf. John 4:25). She went and witnessed about Jesus and many heard of him and knew that Jesus was indeed the Christ, the Savior of the world and believed.

"And said unto the woman, Now we believe, not because of thy saying: for we have heard him ourselves, and know that this is indeed the Christ, the Saviour of the world" (John 4:42)

Can we see the plan of God to save even Gentiles besides Jews His own people? Thanks to God that we, who are Gentiles, are saved by His grace.

SECTION V
THE SALVATION MESSAGES

CHAPTER 29
THE HEAD CORNER STONE

"The stone which the builders refused is become the head stone of the corner" (Psalms 118:22)

Peter and John, the disciples of Jesus Christ, preached the Gospel and the resurrection from the dead. They healed an impotent man in the name of Jesus. Their ministry was blessed and the number of believers increased from three thousand to five thousand. This kind of preaching, and miracles, in the name of Jesus, grieved the high priest Annas, Caiaphas, and Alexander, who thought that the preaching belonged to them, and there is no resurrection from the dead.

Sadducees did not believe in the resurrection, and as they were against this teaching they laid hands on Peter and John, the disciples of Jesus, for a trial the next day. The elders, scribes, Annas, the high priest and high priest's kindred gathered at Jerusalem and questioned the authority by which they healed the impotent man, and preached the resurrection from the dead. Peter, then, filled with Holy Spirit, spoke to them and said to them very firmly that they preached and healed the impotent man in the name of Jesus Christ of Nazareth, whom they crucified, and whom God raised from the dead.

Jesus is the stone, who these elders, Pharisees, Sadducees rejected, but God set him as the Chief corner stone. David prophesied about Jesus, who was the stone, that the builders rejected, yet the LORD made him the head stone of the corner.

"And have ye not read this scripture; The stone which the builders rejected is become the head of the corner" (Mark 12:10)

Peter and John, the disciples of Jesus, who walked with him, witnessed that Jesus was the stone, whom the Jews rejected, but he became the head stone of the corner. They affirm that there is no other name under heaven where anyone can find salvation.

One may object to this preaching but the Bible says it very firmly that there is no salvation except by believing that Jesus is the Savior. Peter and John, the Apostles, who were not learned, or educated, boldly said these things because they were with Jesus and took knowledge from him, who is the only begotten Son of God. The accusers attempted to execute the disciples of Jesus but did not find any cause to punish them, and let them go.

"Unto you therefore which believe he is precious: but unto them which be disobedient, the stone which the builders disallowed, the same is made the head of the corner" (1 Peter 2:7) [Cf. Acts 4:1-14, Ps 118:21-23. Isa. 28:16, Ro 9:33, Eph 2:20, 1Pe 2:7]

When Jesus was on the cross He uttered "the seven sayings" and they are:

1.Father forgive them; for they know no what they do (Luke 23:34)
2.Woman behold thy son... behold they mother (John 19:26,27)
3.Today shalt thou be with me in Paradise (Luke 23:43)
4.My God, My God why hast thou forsaken me (Matt. 27:41)
5.I thirst (John 19:28)
6.It is finished (John 19:30)

7.Father, into thy hands I commend my Spirit (Luke 23:46)

The seven utterances of Lord Jesus on the cross had different but essential messages. Not every one of the seven sayings was similar to each other.

The first saying was a prayer to the Father pleading Him to forgive those who scourged and crucified Him. The Lord said in His words "Father forgive them; for they know no what they do (Luke 23:34). Then, He said to His Father that He had manifested the Father's name to the disciples, who were chosen from out of the world and given to Him. They belonged to the Father and He gave them to the Son, and they kept the Father's word.

"I have manifested thy name unto the men which thou gavest me out of the world: thine they were, and thou gavest them me; and they have kept thy word" (John 17:6)

The second saying of the Lord was to His earthly mother that hid disciple John would take care of her after He is gone and said "Behold thy son"; and then, the Lord turned immediately to His disciple John and said to Him "Behold thy mother"; thus fulfilling a vital responsibility of taking care of His earthy mother.

The third saying of the Lord was to show His divine power to forgive sins of man, even as He was on the cross. One of the thieves, who derided the Lord, lost the opportunity of being saved, while the second thief, who confessed that Jesus is the Lord, was given a firm assurance by the Lord that the said thief will be in paradise with the Lord the same day as the Lord would be. The Lord said: "And he said to him, "Truly, I say to you, today you will be with me in Paradise." (Luke 23:43 ESV)

AMID PERSECUTIONS

The Jews demanded that Jesus be crucified and cried "crucify him, crucify him".

"But they cried, saying, Crucify him, crucify him" (Luke 23:21)

Pilate conceding to their request gave sentence that Jesus be crucified. Even though the Jews cried out that Jesus be crucified, they did not physically write the sentence that the Lord should be crucified. It was Pilate who wrote the sentence that Jesus be crucified. It was Herod who did not do justice to the Lord.

"And Pilate gave sentence that it should be as they required" (Luke 23:24)

The Jews paid heavy price for calling upon them and their children the blood of the Lord and for crying that Jesus be crucified.

"Then answered all the people, and said, His blood be on us, and on our children" (Matthew 27:25)

That is the reason why Peter said in His message that they should repent of their sins and receive salvation because they did it in their ignorance.

"But ye denied the Holy One and the Just, and desired a murderer to be granted unto you; And killed the Prince of life, whom God hath raised from the dead; whereof we are witnesses. And his name through faith in his name hath made this man strong, whom ye see and know: yea, the faith which is by him hath given him this perfect soundness in the presence of you all. And now, brethren, I wot that through ignorance ye did it, as did also your rulers. But those things, which God before had shewed by the mouth of all his prophets, that Christ should suffer, he hath so fulfilled. Repent ye therefore, and be converted, that your sins may be blotted out, when the times of refreshing shall come from the presence of the Lord; And he shall send Jesus Christ, which before was preached unto you" (Acts 3:14-20)

The fourth saying of Jesus on the cross was a cry in the form of complaining to the Father as to why the latter forsook the Lord. The Lord took upon Himself our sin and became sin for us. He was paying price on the cross for our sin. It was the time when the Father was judging our sin that was upon the Son on the cross. Although the Trinity is inseparable, yet Jesus in His human form suffered as forsaken (cf. Matthew 27:45-46)

The fifth saying of Jesus on the cross when, after fulfilling all that He came to fulfill, said "I thirst", but He was given a sour vinegar, which He tasted and felt it bad.

The sixth saying of Jesus on the cross was "It is finished". It was a cry of a winner, who accomplished His purpose of coming into this world.

The seventh saying of Jesus on the cross was "Father, into thy hands I commend my Spirit". It was the cry of a winner after having successfully accomplished all the tasks given by the Father. He died on behalf of sinners in order that they may have life by accepting Him as Savior. He was buried and His body did not suffer corruption. He was raised by God on the third day from the dead, and after forty days of appearance to many He ascended into heaven. He is seated, now at the right hand of the Majesty, pleading on our behalf; and will come soon to take His bride, which is the Church.

CHAPTER 30
"FATHER FORGIVE THEM..."

Father forgive them; for they know no what they do (Luke 23:34)

"I have manifested thy name unto the men which thou gavest me out of the world: thine they were, and thou gavest them me; and they have kept thy word" (John 17:6)

The intercessory prayer recorded in John Chapter 17 is indeed great. There are few similarities seen in the intercessory prayers of Moses and Lord Jesus Christ, yet Moses was human and Lord Jesus Christ is the "Son of God".

Moses was son of Hebrew Parents, of the tribe of Levi. He chose a life of hardship in order to save God's chosen people, his own kinsmen, Israelites. Moses escaped the wrath of Pharaoh, when he chose to rescue his brethren. His life span lasted for 120 years, divided in to forty equal parts of very fruitful years. First set of forty years were of his growth from his childhood to an young man, second set of forty years constituted his earthly life, third set of forty years forty years were dedicated by him for the deliverance of his own brethren, from the bondage of slavery under Pharaoh, and led them to the Promised land of Canaan. He became leader after eighty years and spent forty years of fruitful years as a leader; nevertheless he once took his own decision outside the will of God resulting in being denied to enter into the Promised Land.

"Because ye trespassed against me among the children of Israel at the waters of Meribah-Kadesh, in the wilderness of Zin; because ye sanctified me not in the midst of the children of

Israel. Yet thou shalt see the land before thee; but thou shalt not go thither unto the land which I give the children of Israel" (Deuteronomy 32:51-52)

It was to enter the promised land of Canaan, which was denied to him, because of his choice of making his own will prevail upon God's will. God wrote the Ten Commandments on two tablets with his own finger and gave to Moses to deliver them to the children of Israel but when he came down from Mount Sinai after having direct conversation with God he saw the children of God worshipping idols of manmade gods. Moses got furious and broke down the tablets containing the Ten Commandments. Once he struck the rock to fetch water at "Horeb" according to God's will but next time in order to fetch water in the wilderness of Zin, he took his own decision of striking the rock instead of speaking to it (Ref: Numbers 20:8, 11)

God gave him second time, the same Ten Commandments, which he preserved in the 'Tabernacle'. Moses wrote Torah, which constituted the five books, namely, Genesis, Exodus, Leviticus, Numbers and Deuteronomy. Moses died a natural death.

"Giving thanks unto the Father, which hath made us meet to be partakers of the inheritance of the saints in light: Who hath delivered us from the power of darkness, and hath translated us into the kingdom of his dear Son: In whom we have redemption through his blood, even the forgiveness of sins: Who is the image of the invisible God, the firstborn of every creature" (Colossians 1:12-15)

Lord Jesus Christ was the 'Lamb of God' as John the Baptist pointed in John 1:36 and he was without any blemish

(Ephesians 5:27, 1 Peter 1:19) and He was without any sin (Hebrews 4:15) and yet it pleased the Father to bruise Him for our sins (Isaiah 53:10) and was made to be sin for us that we might be made the righteousness of God in Him (2 Corinthians 5:21)

Lord Jesus Christ prayed for forgiveness of the very people who were crucifying him and He forgives the sins of everyone who confesses his sins to Him.

"Then said Jesus, Father, forgive them; for they know not what they do. And they parted his raiment, and cast lots" (Luke 23:34)

When Jesus therefore saw his mother, and the disciple standing by, whom he loved, he saith unto his mother, Woman, behold thy son! Then saith he to the disciple, Behold thy mother! And from that hour that disciple took her unto his own home. (John 19:26-27)

CHAPTER 31
BEHOLD THY SON

One of the seven sayings of Jesus on the cross was:

"Behold thy son"... and he continued saying ... "Behold thy mother"

When Jesus therefore saw his mother, and the disciple standing by, whom he loved, he saith unto his mother, Woman, behold thy son! Then saith he to the disciple, Behold thy mother! And from that hour that disciple took her unto his own home. (John 19:26-27)

When Jesus was in human form having relinquished his glory to become one like us He honored his mother. When he was hung on the cross he gave the responsibility, to one of his disciples John, to look after his mother. Likewise Jesus also comforted his mother that his disciple John, whom he loved, would be her son from then onwards. Jesus showed great love towards everybody on this earth. His love included healing, forgiving sins, and bearing our sins upon himself.

Jesus was the Son of God, who had divine nature in himself while on this earth, in addition to having human nature. He replied to his mother, once, that he came into this world to do His Father's business.

The Father's business in him and through him was to glorify the Father's name and accept crucifixion bearing our sins upon him in order to redeem us from the bondage of sin. His Father's business was more important for him, but he did not neglect his responsibilities while he was on this earth. Mary the earthly mother of Jesus and Joseph did not find him after their one day's journey while returning from Jerusalem to their native place Galilee. They had been to Jerusalem to celebrate Passover feast.

They supposed that Jesus, who was then a twelve-year old boy, was in their company but having not found him in their company they returned to Jerusalem and found him sitting in the temple learning in the midst of doctors, hearing and asking them questions. They did not find him until three days past and when they found him they were surprised to see that all who heard him were astonished at his understanding and answers. They were all amazed. At this time Mary, as a human, and concern for him, asked Jesus why he dealt with them in that way and said she and Joseph were seeking for him with sorrow. (Luke 2:44-48) It is at that time that Jesus replied to her saying, "And he said unto them, How is it that ye sought me? wist ye not that I must be about my Father's business?" (Luke 2:49)

But when he was breathing his last on the cross having taken up on himself our sins, he said to his mother, "Behold thy son" and to his disciple John, whom he loved he said "Behold thy mother" Jesus fulfilled every responsibility that was given to him upon this earth before he died for our sake. He was buried and rose on the third day. Later, he ascended into heaven and seated on the right hand of the Majesty. He promised that all those who have accepted him as their savior will have everlasting life and be with him for ever and ever.

CHAPTER 32
TODAY SHALT THOU BE WITH ME IN PARADISE

"And he said to him, "Truly, I say to you, today you will be with me in Paradise." (Luke 23:43 ESV)

"And Pilate gave sentence that it should be as they required" (Luke 23:24)

Pontius Pilate, the governor, conceded to the requirement of Jews and others and proclaimed death sentence upon Jesus in spite of the fact that Jesus did no wrong to anyone. Herod, and Pilate had declared that Jesus was "just" and yet they did not set Him free.

Pilate released a notable criminal, whose name was Barabbas, charged with murder and sedition, from prison, as a gift unto the Jews and gave out the illegal verdict that Jesus be crucified as they required. Barabbas, the noted criminal was released in preference to Jesus, who was perfect and holy, without any blemish and any sin; so much for the injustice of the rulers, who gave illegal sentence, and so much for Jews who called upon themselves the curse that the blood of Jesus be upon them.

"Then answered all the people, and said, His blood be on us, and on our children" (Matthew 27:25)

That fulfils the prophecy.

"He is despised and rejected of men; a man of sorrows, and acquainted with grief: and we hid as it were our faces from him; he was despised, and we esteemed him not" (Isaiah 53:3)

AMID PERSECUTIONS

As Jesus was being led away they forced one whose name was Simon, a Cyrenian, who came out of the country, to bear the cross after Jesus. A great company of people, which included women, cried looking at the agony Jesus, who was on His way of fulfilling the prophecies written about seven hundred years ago by Isaiah.

Looking at them the Lord admonished them not to cry for Him but cry for themselves and their children, who required that He be crucified. He said those in future who do not give birth to children will be considered blessed and those who would have children will cry out to the mountains to fall on them and hills to cover them.

The Lord wondered if such great injustice could be done to Him when He was with them, how much would be done in the days when He would not be with them (cf. Matthew 24:19; Luke 21:23; Revelation 6:16-17; Isaiah 2:21). Jesus spoke a proverb that infers that He was as innocent as the green tree in the proverb.

"For if they do these things in a green tree, what shall be done in the dry?" (Luke 23:31)

After this the authorities sent two others, who were criminals, to be put to death with Jesus. How ignominious and hideous it was that the "Just" Lord was considered by them to be equal with two malefactors. A prophecy in Isaiah was fulfilled.

"...and he was numbered with the transgressors; and he bare the sin of many, and made intercession for the transgressors" (Isaiah 53:12b)

AMID PERSECUTIONS

When they reached a place called "Calvary" or "Golgotha" they crucified Jesus along with the two criminals, one on His right and another on the left. In spite of all the injustice they did to Jesus, the Lord prayed to the Father saying ""Father, forgive them, for they know not what they do." And they cast lots and divided his garments in fulfillment of prophecy (Isaiah 53:12a).

The people who were watching scoffed at Him saying "He saved others; let him save himself, if he is the Christ of God, his Chosen One!" If Jesus really wanted to save Himself, he could have prayed and called for legions of angels to fight on behalf of Him, but it was not the purpose that Jesus came into this world for.

"Do you think that I cannot appeal to my Father, and he will at once send me more than twelve legions of angels?" (Matthew 26:53 ESV)

Apostle Paul writes about Jesus:

"Who, being in the form of God, thought it not robbery to be equal with God: But made himself of no reputation, and took upon him the form of a servant, and was made in the likeness of men: And being found in fashion as a man, he humbled himself, and became obedient unto death, even the death of the cross. Wherefore God also hath highly exalted him, and given him a name which is above every name: That at the name of Jesus every knee should bow, of things in heaven, and things in earth, and things under the earth" (Philippians 2:6-10)

The Lord came down die on behalf of sinners that they might have everlasting life by accepting Him as the Lord. One of the soldiers went offering the Lord sour wine and said "If you are the King of the Jews, save yourself!" There was an inscription on the Cross that read ""This is the King of the Jews."

One of the malefactors, who were on the cross, insulted Jesus saying "Are you not the Christ? Save yourself and us!" However, the second malefactor realized that Jesus was the Son of God and the Lord will come as king and establish His kingdom.

The second malefactor then, rebuked the first one and said to him to fear God. He said they received death sentence to die on the cross because they deserved such condemnation, whereas the Lord did no wrong, yet He was under the same condemnation as they were.

Turning to the Lord the second malefactor said "Jesus, remember me when you come into your kingdom." Lord Jesus took compassion on him and said "Truly, I say to you, today you will be with me in Paradise." (cf. Luke 23:32-43 ESV)

Few important points to note here are that Pilate sentenced Jesus to death even though the Lord did no wrong; much less anything that deserved death penalty. Lord Jesus had no blemish in Him. He did not sin neither did He any harm to anyone. He came to save sinners, and did all the good for mankind, and not only He healed the sick, but prayed to the Father to forgive them that crucified Him.

Roman Government treated Jesus one equal with two criminals even though Jesus did not commit any crime.

One of the two malefactors was rude and rash to the Lord and insulted him but the second one confessed that he and other malefactor justly received reward for their wrong doing. He confessed that Jesus is the Lord and that He would come as King to establish His kingdom. He then prayed to the Lord to remember Him when He comes in His glory as King.

Lord Jesus was not only compassionate to forgive the sins of the second malefactor immediately but He assured him that he would be with the Lord in Paradise the same day.

Salvation is as simple confessing by mouth that Jesus is Lord and believe in heart He was raised from the dead on the third day. Today is the day to confess your sins to Jesus and accept Him as your Lord if you wish to receive everlasting life; otherwise, according to the Bible, the place of those who are not saved is the "lake of fire".

CHAPTER 33
ELI, ELI, LAMA SABACHTHANI

(My God, my God, why hast thou forsaken me?)
From Matthew 27:46

"Now from the sixth hour there was darkness over all the land unto the ninth hour. And about the ninth hour Jesus cried with a loud voice, saying, Eli, Eli, lama sabachthani? that is to say, My God, my God, why hast thou forsaken me?" (Matthew 27:45-46)

From the sixth hour of the day in Jerusalem until the ninth of hour there, which is equivalent to 12.00 PM to 3.00 PM of our time, there was utter darkness on the face of the earth when Jesus was on the cross, bearing our sin upon Himself.

It pleased the Father to bruise His Son Jesus for our sin (cf. prophecy in Isaiah 53:10), and our sin was judged at the cross by the righteous Lord God.

"Yet it pleased the LORD to bruise him; he hath put him to grief: when thou shalt make his soul an offering for sin, he shall see his seed, he shall prolong his days, and the pleasure of the LORD shall prosper in his hand" (Isaiah 53:10)

It was at that time that the Father brought about severest darkness on the face of the earth. Jesus took our punishment on Himself and our sin on Him was judged at the Cross. The Father, the Holy One, could not see the sin on the Son Jesus Christ, and that is the reason why the Father judged the sin at the cross where Lord Jesus was hung bearing our sin. Darkness signifies judgment and during this darkness our sin was judged at the Cross.

"For he hath made him to be sin for us, who knew no sin; that we might be made the righteousness of God in him" (2 Corinthians 5:21)

"Christ hath redeemed us from the curse of the law, being made a curse for us: for it is written, Cursed is every one that hangeth on a tree" (Galatians 3:13)

"his body shall not remain all night on the tree, but you shall bury him the same day, for a hanged man is cursed by God. You shall not defile your land that the LORD your God is giving you for an inheritance" (Deuteronomy 21:23 ESV)

Jesus, who knew no sin, was made sin for us in order that we might be made the righteousness of God in Him. There are contentious beliefs that Father can look upon the sin of man, and therefore, Jesus was not forsaken; but considering the fact that sin is pernicious, heinous, offensive and polluted, it is hardly believable that the Holy Father God could see sin upon the Son of God.

In the Old Testament according to the Law, Moses was commanded by the LORD, to burn the bullock, and his hide, his flesh and his dung outside the camp. This shadow was fulfilled in Jesus when the sin on Him was judged at Golgotha, outside the city, in order that He may become propitiation and die a substitutionary death on behalf of us to redeem us to give us everlasting life. Anyone can receive this everlasting life by believing that Jesus is the Lord and God raised Him from the dead.

"But the bullock, and his hide, his flesh, and his dung, he burnt with fire without the camp; as the LORD commanded Moses" (Leviticus 8:17)

It was neither an eclipse nor was the usual darkness that came at sunset, but it was utter darkness from noon to three past noon. It was during the Passover that this darkness came upon the face of the earth and this darkness prevailed on the face of the earth in the midst of the day light. It was indeed unusual.

"Verily, verily, I say unto you, He that heareth my word, and believeth on him that sent me, hath everlasting life, and shall not come into condemnation; but is passed from death unto life". (John 5:24)

Darkness was one of the ten plagues that God brought on Egypt. "And the LORD said unto Moses, Stretch out thine hand toward heaven, that there may be darkness over the land of Egypt, even darkness [which] may be felt. And Moses stretched forth his hand toward heaven; and there was a thick darkness in all the land of Egypt three days" Exodus 10:21,22

"And it came between the camp of the Egyptians and the camp of Israel; and it was a cloud and darkness to them, but it gave light by night to these: so that the one came not near the other all the night". (Exodus 14:20)

Darkness is accompanied with fear, sin, and judgment. It is opposed to luster and honor. It is opposed to wisdom; it is associated with confusion, folly, vexation of Spirit, and calamities. An angel shone light towards Israelites when Israelites were just about to cross Red Sea, and darkness to Pharaoh and his army. It was the judgment that Pharaoh and his army were about to face while the children of God were about to cross the Red Sea.

Scriptures speak of the sun and the moon getting fully darkened, and the stars withdrawing their shining in the last days. It happens when the Lord comes again to this earth.

"The sun and the moon shall be darkened, and the stars shall withdraw their shining". (Joel 3:15)

When Jesus was on the cross he quoted directly from Psalm 22:1 and cried aloud "Eli, Eli, lama sabachthani? that is to say, My God, my God, why hast thou forsaken me?"

"My God, my God, why hast thou forsaken me? why art thou so far from helping me, and from the words of my roaring?" (Psalms 22:1)

Although the details of separation or non-separation of the Father and the Son at the cross, for a while, are known to the Father and the Son only, yet it is worth considering, to the best of our knowledge, whether or not the Son was forsaken at the Lord's death and why Lord Jesus said "My God, my God, why hast thou forsaken me?" It is necessary that we understand what exactly happened during those dark hours, and the way the Father judged sin upon the Son.

Lord Jesus had two natures in His incarnation when He relinquished His glory that He had with the Father and came into this world in the form of a servant and in the likeness of man. One nature that He had was of divine and the other of human. He felt the human traits such as joy, pain, sadness, hunger. He wept at the tomb of Lazarus, who was dead for four days. However, the pain He suffered at the cross was, indeed, much more in its intensity. He bore our sin and took the penalty of our sin upon Himself and paid for our sin and punishment. It was not by silver or by gold that we were redeemed but by His precious blood, and therefore, the cost of our redemption was very heavy.

Lord Jesus felt separation from the Father just as the David felt separation from God but the Lord was not forsaken to be our savior or ceased to be God. He was for a short while, in His human nature, felt all alone while our sin was on Him. God is Almighty, who is triune, and who lives forever and ever, is inseparable. God is omnipresent, omniscient, and omnipotent.

"Thus saith the LORD, The heaven is my throne, and the earth is my footstool: where is the house that ye build unto me? and where is the place of my rest?" (Isaiah 66:1)

It would also be apt to consider here whether or not David felt separation from God when He cried "My God, my God, why hast thou forsaken me? why art thou so far from helping me, and from the words of my roaring?" (Psalms 22:1)

The caption of the Psalm is "To the chief Musician upon Aijeleth Shahar, A Psalm of David" David was singing a song extemporarily, an unknown tune, pointing to Lord Jesus Christ's sufferings than to himself. It was an unknown future to him. When He sang the song He neither felt Jesus would be separated from the Father or not but He said "My God, my God why hast thou forsaken me" in prophecy. The psalm is Messianic. He did not mean Jesus would be separated or would not be separated; however the word meaning of "forsaken" is abandon.

David lost fellowship with God when He had illegal relationship with Bathsheba and got her husband Uriah killed. His sin did not go unpunished. God dealt with Him severely but taking away his firstborn son, and putting him to terrible ignominy (Ref. 2 Samuel 12:1-19).

Similarly when Jesus was on the cross He, in His human nature was bearing our sin and that sin was judged severely by the Father and Jesus felt separation from the Father; however God raised Him from the dead and said to Him "You are my Son, today I have begotten you".

So also Christ did not exalt himself to be made a high priest, but was appointed by him who said to him, "You are my Son, today I have begotten you"; (Hebrews 5:5 ESV)

Psalmist goes on singing the song indicating the Lord's exaltation in His future kingdom. He concludes the psalm in praises and the Lord's exaltation as the King.

"All the prosperous of the earth eat and worship; before him shall bow all who go down to the dust, even the one who could not keep himself alive. Posterity shall serve him; it shall be told of the Lord to the coming generation; they shall come and proclaim his righteousness to a people yet unborn, that he has done it" (Psalm 22:29-31 ESV)

Lord Jesus said:

"I and my Father are one". (John 10:30)

Although the word "forsaken" in Hebrew, Greek and in English means "abandon" Lord Jesus Christ was not forsaken eternally, but He felt separation from the Father, because He was bearing our sin upon Himself, and that is why He was quoting from Psalm 22:1 when He cried "My God, my God, why hast thou forsaken me?"

"And about the ninth hour Jesus cried with a loud voice, saying, Eli, Eli, lama sabachthani? that is to say, My God, my God, why hast thou forsaken me?" (Matthew 27:46)

Let us worship the Father in the name of our Lord and Savior Jesus Christ, who was crucified, died for our sake, was buried and was raised from the dead on the third day. Jesus ascended into heaven and he is seated on the right hand of the Majesty.

CHAPTER 34
I THIRST

After this, Jesus knowing that all things were now accomplished, that the scripture might be fulfilled, saith, I thirst. (John 19:28)

According to medical science "thirst" is the craving for fluids. Thirst arises in living beings as a result of fluid levels falling down below the normal levels. The brain sends signals to desire for fluids and drink them in order that vital body functions may not become dysfunctional. Continual lack of supply of fluids to the cells in the body will result in dehydration, and functions of vital organs such as kidneys to become dysfunctional resulting in death.

Why did the Son of God, Lord Jesus thirst? Although Jesus was divine, He also had human nature in Him when He was on this earth. He was fully divine and fully human.

On His incarnation and while descending from heaven to the earth, in human form, He voluntarily relinquished His glory that He had with the Father, and took upon a form of servant, in the likeness of man. No man could do any harm to Him until He voluntarily became a sacrifice for us in order that we may receive salvation. Salvation is available for anyone who seeks for it, free of cost.

When a man is thirsty and does not receive water to drink, and instead receives unsavory drink, he surely feels frustrated. However, when Lord Jesus was on the cross, he did not chide anyone for doing any wrong to Him any time; not even when soldiers and one of the two thieves mocked at Him; rather He said "Father forgive them for they do not know what they do".

AMID PERSECUTIONS

It would be so comforting and soothing if we receive water when we are thirsty; however, when the creator of this universe did not receive water in response His craving for water when He said "I thirst", He received from them "a jar full of sour wine stood there, so they put a sponge full of the sour wine on a hyssop branch and held it to his mouth". He tasted it and found it unsavory.

Lord Jesus lived among people and healed the sick, forgave them their sin, and helped in their needs and yet they insulted Him, scourged Him, and spat upon His face. They put upon His head a crown of thorns and mocked saying "King of the Jews". There were no thorns when God created the earth, but the thorns grew as a result of man's disobedience (cf. Gen 3:18). Here, the crown of thorns represents that curse which He took upon Himself, on behalf of us.

Jesus bore our sin upon Himself when He was on the cross as a sacrificial "Lamb of God" to purge our sins, and later sit at the right hand of the Majesty. He was in agony on the cross and craved for water, but no man found sympathy towards Him. He accomplished the purpose and the prophecies were fulfilled. This is unique about Christianity that Jesus came into this world according to prophecies and died and rose from the dead according to prophecies. There was no way man could get salvation unless He died on behalf of sinners, by taking upon Himself the sin of every man in this world.

There is neither salvation available by doing good works and in any other man. There was never a god who came to die for the sins of others; much less fulfilling any prophecy and much less rising from the dead and ascending into heaven. Good works follow salvation but they are not the means to attain salvation.

AMID PERSECUTIONS

God works deserve appreciation but they can never save a man from escaping from the "lake of fire". The only way to escape from being thrown into hell-fire is to accept Lord Jesus Christ as personal Savior.

If we say we have no sin in us or we have no sin in our selves we make God a liar. The Bible says everyone has sinned and come short of the glory. We have all gone astray and need savior. While we were yet sinners, being enemies of God, and without any strength, He died on behalf of us and that is God's love. It is by grace through faith that we are saved.

For when we were yet without strength, in due time Christ died for the ungodly. For scarcely for a righteous man will one die: yet peradventure for a good man some would even dare to die. But God commendeth his love toward us, in that, while we were yet sinners, Christ died for us. (Romans 5:6-8)

He said "I thirst". The Lord not only bore our griefs and our sorrows, but He also took upon Himself our sin that we might be made righteous by accepting Him as the Lord.

It was a cry of the Lord, who was triumphant over Satan by judging sin on the cross, and yet they gave Him vinegar and thus the prophecies were fulfilled.

"They gave me also gall for my meat; and in my thirst they gave me vinegar to drink". (Psalms 69:21)

"Surely he has borne our griefs and carried our sorrows; yet we esteemed him stricken, smitten by God, and afflicted. But he was pierced for our transgressions; he was crushed for our iniquities; upon him was the chastisement that brought us peace, and with his wounds we are healed" (Isaiah 53:4-5 ESV)

It is time now time for those of us, who are not saved, to repent of their sins and accept Jesus as their Savior and believe in heart that God raised Him from the dead.

"For he hath made him to be sin for us, who knew no sin; that we might be made the righteousness of God in him" (2 Corinthians 5:21)

CHAPTER 35
IT IS FINISHED

"When Jesus therefore had received the vinegar, he said, It is finished: and he bowed his head, and gave up the ghost" (John 19:30)

After five utterances that Jesus made on the cross, the phrase "It is finished" is the sixth one that He uttered. This utterance has come to be known as the sixth saying. (cf. John 19:30a).

The word "finished" is a translation from Greek word "teleo" (Strong's Number 5055), which means "paid in full". It is a legal accounting term used when the dues are paid in full. Inasmuch as man became a debtor to God by sinning against Him, it was necessary that he be reconciled to God. There was only one way for man to be reconciled to God, and it was by shedding blood on behalf of sinner and the scripture says "...without the shedding of blood there is no forgiveness of sins" (cf. Hebrews 9:21-22b ESV).

As the Old Testament Laws and sacrifices were not enough to provide atonement of sins of mankind, the only way available for mankind to be reconciled to God, was for the Son of God to come into this world and die on behalf of man.

"For God so loved the world, that he gave his only begotten Son, that whosoever believeth in him should not perish, but have everlasting life" (John 3:16)

It was a debt that only the Son of God could pay; and Lord Jesus Christ paid the price of our sin by shedding His blood upon the cross. Jesus came into this world and died on behalf of us and rose from the dead on the third day.

Thus, Lord Jesus redeemed us from the bondage of sin; but then salvation is available for man only by accepting Jesus as Lord and by believing in heart that God raised Him from the dead on the third day.

Lord Jesus suffered on the cross on behalf of us, and yet it was a cry of a winner, who came into this world with a definite purpose of fulfilling the desire of the Father. It is the cry of the winner, who accomplished all that He was to do on this earth, according to the wishes of the Father.

Lord Jesus came into this world

1. To glorify the Father on the earth (John 5:36-37; John 12:28; John 17:4)
2. To seek that which was lost (Luke19:10)
3. To Provide atonement of sins (Romans 3:23-25)
4. To Reconcile man to God (2 Corinthians 5:18-21)
5. To fulfill prophecies; the first one being Genesis 3:15
6. To be the obedient servant (Isaiah 53)
7. To Provide shield of faith to quench the flaming arrows of the evil (Ephesians 6:16)
8. To Quicken (Ephesians 2:1,5)
9. To pave the way for unification of Jews and Gentiles (Ephesians 3:6)

At the pool of Bethesda He healed, on a Sabbath day, an invalid man who was lying there for thirty eight years. Jews, who were staunch followers of Mosaic Law, took objection to such healing on the Sabbath day. Jesus was doing that which was good for man and He was the Lord of the Sabbath.

"For the Son of man is Lord even of the sabbath day" (Matthew 12:8)

Not only the Lord healed the man on the Sabbath, but He said He was doing the works of His Father. "But Jesus answered them, "My Father is working until now, and I am working." (John 5:17 ESV)

The Jews sought to kill Him because He not only healed the man on the Sabbath day, but He also called God as His Father. Thus Jesus exalted and glorified the Father all through His ministry on this earth. He came to seek that which was lost. He came to reconcile man to God. He came to pay the price of our sin and to fulfill the prophecies of Old Testament, the first of which, He being the seed of the woman, was to crush the seed of the serpent and He did it on the cross by defeating Satan. It pleased the Father to bruise Him on the cross in order that we might receive salvation by accepting Jesus as the Savior.

"Yet it pleased the LORD to bruise him; he hath put him to grief: when thou shalt make his soul an offering for sin, he shall see his seed, he shall prolong his days, and the pleasure of the LORD shall prosper in his hand" (Isaiah 53:10)

Lord Jesus Christ did not exalt Himself to be made a High priest but the Father declared Him as "You are my Son". Jesus delivered us from the bondage of sin and became High Priest and the mediator between God and man. There is, therefore, no other mediator needed now to approach the Father in heaven.

"Forasmuch then as the children are partakers of flesh and blood, he also himself likewise took part of the same; that through death he might destroy him that had the power of death, that is, the devil; And deliver them who through fear of death were all their lifetime subject to bondage" (Hebrews 2:14-15)

"So also Christ did not exalt himself to be made a high priest, but was appointed by him who said to him, 'You are my Son, today I have begotten you'; " (Hebrews 5:5 ESV)

CHAPTER 36
"...FATHER, INTO THY HANDS I COMMEND MY SPIRIT"

"And when Jesus had cried with a loud voice, he said, Father, into thy hands I commend my spirit: and having said thus, he gave up the ghost" (Luke 23:46)

The seventh saying of Jesus on the cross was "Father, into thy hands I commend my spirit" and then He gave up His Spirit in the Father's hands on His volition. Centurion gave testimony of Jesus. No one in the world, whether he be considered as god or human, gave up his life by his own volition, except committing suicide.

"Now when the centurion saw what was done, he glorified God, saying, Certainly this was a righteous man" (Luke 23:47)

People who saw Jesus die on the cross smote their breasts and returned. Those who were acquainted with Him and the woman, who followed Him from Galilee, stood far off looking at these things (cf. Luke 23:44-49)

There was never such a humiliating death one was subjected to, such as Jesus was subjected to, during the Roman Government period or under any Government. He did nothing that deserved death penalty, yet He was condemned to death by crucifixion.

The usual custom during those days was that the person on the cross will be left alone until he loses his life; but when Jesus and two other thieves were crucified on the cross, one on His right and the other on His left, giving an impression that Jesus was equal with those two thieves, it was Passover day and the next day was Sabbath day".

According to Mosaic Law the dead body should not remain on the cross on the Sabbath day (cf. Deut. 21: 22-23; John 19:31). Therefore, soldiers came and broke the legs of the two thieves but when they came to Jesus, they found Him dead already, and therefore, they did not break His legs, thus fulfilling the prophecy.

For these things were done, that the scripture should be fulfilled, A bone of him shall not be broken. (John 19:36)

"He keepeth all his bones: not one of them is broken" (Psalms 34:20)

The curtain in the temple was torn into two from top to bottom, revealing that Jews and Gentiles are one and everyone has access to the Holy One through Jesus Christ the mediator (cf. Exodus 26:31; Leviticus 16:2; 21:23; 2Chronicles 3:14; Matt. 27:51; Hebrews 10:20)

Jesus was the winner at the cross and His cry on the cross showed us His intimacy with the Father, who sent Him into this world with a mission; and Jesus fulfilled the mission. It was a cry of the winner, who relinquished His glory with the Father and came down in the form of a servant and in the likeness of man to die on behalf of us and rise from the dead, in order that we may, by accepting Him, as the Lord and by believing in heart that God raised Him from the dead on the third day, might become righteous. Our righteousness was like filthy rags before God and although our sins were like scarlet they were made as white as wool.

"We have all become like one who is unclean, and all our righteous deeds are like a polluted garment. We all fade like a leaf, and our iniquities, like the wind, take us away" (Isaiah 64:6 ESV)

"Come now, let us reason together, says the LORD: though your sins are like scarlet, they shall be as white as snow; though they are red like crimson, they shall become like wool. (Isaiah 1:18 ESV)

Who can by his/her efforts can become righteous before God? The word of God says we have all come short of the glory and our righteousness is like filthy rags before God. We cannot save ourselves at any cost, by any means, because man is imperfect and never can he become perfect. Self-humiliation or walking several steps up the stairs made of stone, and reaching after a great struggle the top of a hill, where a deity sat in idol form cannot save us from destruction (cf. Isaiah 44:9) It is by grace through faith in Lord Jesus Christ only that we can be saved from destruction.

Jesus, who was the express image of the Father, and creator of this universe, purged our sins and sat down at the right hand of the Majesty. His body did not see corruption when He was in the grave, and He rose from the dead on the third day; and after forty days He ascended into Heaven. He appeared before many people during the forty days after His resurrection.

Speaking of Jesus, Apostle Paul wrote we have redemption through His blood, even the forgiveness of sins. He is the image of invisible God, the first born of every creature. By Him were all things created that are in heaven, and that are in earth, visible and invisible, whether they be thrones, or dominions, or principalities, or powers.

"In whom we have redemption, the forgiveness of sins. He is the image of the invisible God, the firstborn of all creation. For by him all things were created, in heaven and on earth, visible and invisible, whether thrones or dominions or rulers or authorities—all things were created through him and for him. And he is before all things, and in him all things hold together. And he is the head of the body, the church. He is the beginning, the firstborn from the dead, that in everything he might be preeminent. For in him all the fullness of God was pleased to dwell, and through him to reconcile to himself all things, whether on earth or in heaven, making peace by the blood of his cross. And you, who once were alienated and hostile in mind, doing evil deeds, he has now reconciled in his body of flesh by his death, in order to present you holy and blameless and above reproach before him" (Colossians 1:14-22 ESV)

By His resurrection and in His glorified body, Jesus has shown us that by believing in Him as our savior, we will rise from the dead in glorified body, and will be conformed to His image (cf. Romans 8:29) and then we will say "O death where is thy sting, O grave, where is thy victory"

"So when this corruptible shall have put on incorruption, and this mortal shall have put on immortality, then shall be brought to pass the saying that is written, Death is swallowed up in victory. O death, where is thy sting? O grave, where is thy victory?" (1 Corinthians 15:54-55)

This is the great hope of Christian life. We will live eternally with immortal bodies sans misery, weeping or death any more (Rev 22:1-5), while those who do not believe in Him as savior and depend on their righteousness will end up in "lake of fire", of which the Bible speaks in Revelation 19:20; 20:10; 20:14; 20:15

CHAPTER 37
THE INNER MAN

(FROM EPHESIANS 3:14-21)

In order to understand Paul's usage of the word "inner man" in Ephesians 3:14-21, it is imperative that we know how the words and phrases, such as "flesh", "fleshly desires", "inner man", "carnal", are used in the Scriptures. Everyone has outer body and inner man. The usage of the word "flesh" in Scriptures does not necessarily refer to "sin", but it denotes the body as distinguished from the soul. The following examples will give us the answer that Spirit is different from the body.

"And the LORD said, My spirit shall not always strive with man, for that he also is flesh: yet his days shall be an hundred and twenty years" (Genesis 6:3)

"And the Word was made flesh, and dwelt among us, (and we beheld his glory, the glory as of the only begotten of the Father,) full of grace and truth" (John 1:14)

The phrase "fleshly desires" point to the desires of the flesh leading to sin as a result of evil that comes from the heart. The word "carnal" denotes the corporeal appetites, and corrupt nature of the body as a whole, and fulfilment of fleshly desires leading to sin.

When John wrote "...the Word was made flesh, and dwelt among us" he meant that the Word was made to be a living body and the body in reference was of the Lord Jesus Christ. The Scripture says: "... (and we beheld his glory, the glory as of the only begotten of the Father,) full of grace and truth", and

"Behold, the Lamb of God, who takes away the sin of the world!" (cf. John 1:29; John 1:36)

THE INNER SELF

The "inner man" is the real self, a combination of spirit and soul; and thus man's body consists of outer body, which is flesh, the spirit, which is the breath of life, and the soul is the actual man inside the body.

In this passage Paul lays emphasis on the necessity of regularly strengthening, refreshing of inner man in us by the might of His Spirit. In order that inner man is spiritually nourished it is imperative that we allow Lord Jesus Christ to occupy the whole of our heart rather than conceding limited access.

If we are serious to improve the quality of our Christian life, it is essential that we allow our Lord to control our lives, and cast our entire burden on Him in order that He may take care of us fully. We should give Him full authority to lead our lives. What a great peace and joy it would be to cast upon Him our entire burden in order that He may lead our lives. When He takes charge of our lives and leads us in this world we will overcome the temptations of this world.

ON KNEES WHILE PRAYING

Apostle Paul bows on his knees to the Father of our Lord Jesus Christ and prays for the believers at Ephesus Church, which he planted by the grace of God, that the Lord may grant them, according to the riches of His glory, to be strengthened in the inner man with the might of Holy Spirit.

In all cases of intense meditation before the throne of grace, it is better that we find a place, or close the door of the room, and kneel down and pray to the Lord. As far as possible, and as the situation and time permits, our prerogative should be to bow down on our knees and pray. Nevertheless, our legalistic approach making it mandatory to kneel while praying is wrong. It is the bowing down of the heart to the Lord that matters rather than physical posture that we adopt.

ONE FAMILY

God is our Father, to whom belong all those who have received salvation. We are called the "children of God", as one family whether they are in heaven, or on earth. The children of God as we are, we are entitled to be granted to be strengthened in our inner self, according to the riches of His glory. The outer body deteriorates gradually and ends up in grave. We are made of dust and to dust we will return; yet because we are "born-again" children of God, we will be raised in our spirits, and in our glorified bodies, when the Lord comes again to be with the Lord forever and ever.

FAITH IN THE LORD

Our desire should be to be rooted and grounded in love by faith in Lord Jesus Christ. Our endeavors should be to comprehend, along with all His saints, the breadth, the length, the depth and height of His love. Our deeds falls too short when we understand the true love Lord Jesus Christ shown on the Cross. Lord Jesus bore our sins upon Him and died on behalf of us, in order that salvation may be available for everyone who believes that He is the Lord, and God raised Him from the dead. Escape from hell-fire and receive everlasting life by fulfilling that one criterion.

BREADTH, LENGTH, DEPTH AND THE HEIGHT

"May be able to comprehend with all saints what is the breadth, and length, and depth, and height" (Ephesians 3:18)

Who can fathom God's love towards us? The breadth, the length, the depth, and the height of His love are so inexplicable and unfathomable that He gave His only Son to be crucified on the cross bearing our sin in order that whoever believes in Him shall not perish but have everlasting life. There is neither anyone saved in the past, nor will be saved either in the present generation, or in future except by accepting Jesus as Lord and by believing in heart that God raised Him from the dead.

The mystery of the Church was unknown in the Old Testament, but it is revealed to us. In Christ alone is salvation and every believer, whether he is Jew or Gentile, will see Him face to face and be with the Lord forever and ever.

The Lord has bestowed on us such love that we should be called the sons of God. The world does not know the value of it, because it does not know the Father.

"See what kind of love the Father has given to us, that we should be called children of God; and so we are. The reason why the world does not know us is that it did not know him. Beloved, we are God's children now, and what we will be has not yet appeared; but we know that when he appears we shall be like him, because we shall see him as he is. And everyone who thus hopes in him purifies himself as he is pure" (1 John 3:1-3 ESV)

The mystery of the Church is revealed in Ephesians Chapters 2 and 3. His love is from everlasting to everlasting. We are given the privilege to be joint heirs of His love (cf. John 3:16; 1 Cor. 13:8; Phil.2:8).

"The Spirit himself bears witness with our spirit that we are children of God, and if children, then heirs—heirs of God and fellow heirs with Christ, provided we suffer with him in order that we may also be glorified with him" (Romans 8:16-17 ESV)

INCREASE IN KNOWLEDGE

The Lord desires that we may not remain in the status of babes in Christ our entire life, but to increase in the knowledge of God. It is necessary that we make endeavors to possess the attributes of Lord to have fullness of God, which is to refresh in His knowledge and allow Him to occupy our hearts fully. While making such endeavors it is imperative that we know that God will not share His glory to anyone. God's incommunicable attributes such as "self-existence", "self-sufficient", "immutability" cannot be shared by us and we cannot become equal with God at any time. We have the privilege of sharing His communicable attributes such as "Spirituality", "individuality", "knowledge", "wisdom", "truthfulness".

Paul in his doxology exalts in sublime words that the Lord is able to give us exceedingly and abundantly all that we ask in the Lord's name according to His purposes, and according to the power of Holy Spirt who is at work in us. Unto the Lord is glory in the Church, and in Christ Jesus throughout all ages, world without end. Amen. (cf. Eph. 3:20-21)

It also helps us to recollect how David praised the LORD in Psalm chapter 148, which is full of praises and advices that the entire creation should praise the Him

PRAISE THE NAME OF THE LORD

"Praise the LORD! Praise the LORD from the heavens; praise him in the heights! Praise him, all his angels; praise him, all his hosts! Praise him, sun and moon, praise him, all you shining stars! Praise him, you highest heavens, and you waters above the heavens! Let them praise the name of the LORD! For he commanded and they were created. And he established them forever and ever;   he gave a decree, and it shall not pass away" (Psalm 148:1-6 ESV)

CHAPTER 38
DO WE CARE?

Do we care for the Inner man?

"And the LORD God formed man of the dust of the ground, and breathed into his nostrils the breath of life; and man became a living soul" (Genesis 2:7)

Who is inner man? Man has body, soul and spirit. Soul and spirit constitute the inner man. We all care about the outer man, which is the physical body. Physical body is made of flesh, which is nothing but dust. God made man out of dust and dust that the man is, he will return to dust. When God made man, He breathed His spirit into the nostrils of man, and man became living being. It is because man trespassed against God, the death came upon him and everyone will die once.

"Wherefore, as by one man sin entered into the world, and death by sin; and so death passed upon all men, for that all have sinned" (Romans 5:12)

It is the inner man, which is the combination of soul and spirit that never perishes. It will be either with God after man's physical death, or it will be cast into the "lake of fire", if the man is not reconciled with God. If we take care of our outer bodies, which perish one day, so much to keep it fit by doing exercises and yoga etc., then how much should we care about our inner man that never perishes! Don't we have to think that our inner man lives in the light forever, rather than he is casting into hell-fire?

Let us gather treasures in heaven. Make sure that your soul will be with God in the light, rather than in hell. Bible says what if a man gathers whole world and loses his soul.

"For what is a man profited, if he shall gain the whole world, and lose his own soul? or what shall a man give in exchange for his soul?" (Matthew 16:26)

Salvation can never be achieved by doing good works or by working for it in our way, because we are not perfect, neither we do can make us perfect in the sight of God. All our righteousness is like filthy rags before God.

It is by grace through faith that we are saved. Believe in Jesus in whom alone there is salvation. He gave His life on behalf us that we may have everlasting life by confessing our sins to Him.

"So when this corruptible shall have put on incorruption, and this mortal shall have put on immortality, then shall be brought to pass the saying that is written, Death is swallowed up in victory. O death, where is thy sting? O grave, where is thy victory?" (1 Corinthians 15:54-55)

"For the wages of sin is death; but the gift of God is eternal life through Jesus Christ our Lord" (Romans 6:23)

CHAPTER 39
REWARDS FROM RIGHTEOUS JUDGE

"I have fought a good fight, I have finished my course, I have kept the faith: Henceforth there is laid up for me a crown of righteousness, which the Lord, the righteous judge, shall give me at that day: and not to me only, but unto all them also that love his appearing". (2 Timothy 4:7-8)

At the fag-end of Paul's life when he knew that he would not live anymore, because of his impending execution unto death by Nero for preaching the Gospel, he writes letter to Timothy, whom he called as his son in faith and in Christian ministry, exhorting him to preach the word of God. He recollects his own ministry and says that he fought a good fight, finished his course, and kept the faith. Paul, therefore, says that the Lord Jesus Christ will give him a crown of righteousness at the Judgment seat of Christ. He says not only he receives such crown of righteousness but all those who believe in Lord Jesus Christ and love His second coming.

Indeed, Paul struggled hard to proclaim the Gospel of Lord Jesus Christ from the beginning of his ministry. He had a bad past record of persecuting Christians. His name was Saul before his conversion to Christianity. He had consented to the death of Spirit-filled Stephen and kept the raiment of them that slew him. He threatened to slaughter the disciples of the Lord. He desired letters from high priest to Damascus to the synagogues that if he found any disciples of the Lord, whether be men or women, he would bring them bound to Jerusalem. But then as he journeyed to Damascus he encountered Lord Jesus Christ on the way.

AMID PERSECUTIONS

There shone a great light suddenly from heaven around him. Saul fell down to the ground and he heard a voice asking him "Saul, Saul, why persecutest thou me?" Saul answered and said "Who are thou Lord?" Then the Lord answered him and said "I am Jesus whom thou pesecutest: it is hard for thee to kick against pricks".

It is indeed hard to be obstructive, or stubborn not to believe Jesus as the Lord and fight against His teachings. The ox that kicks against pricks hurts itself and none else. The pricks refereed to here are goads that the farmer uses to prick the ox while farming. The stubborn ox that kicks against such goads, which are sharp iron pieces stuck into the edge of the stick, injures itself and none else.

The Lord was using this phrase against Saul who was persecuting Christians and the disciples. Hurting Christians was like hurting Lord Jesus Christ Himself. Saul was thrown onto the ground and humbled in no time and was made blind. The voice from Lord Jesus Christ was heard by others who were accompanying Saul but they could not see any man. Saul humbled himself immediately.

It is the obedience and change of heart that God demands at a man's conversion to follow Jesus. Then there should be the willingness to accept Lord Jesus Christ as savior. Confessing by mouth the Lord Jesus Christ and believing in heart that God raised Him from the dead will earn salvation and that is called 'born-again'. The salvation is neither earned by gold nor silver or good works but by faith in Him alone.

"That if thou shalt confess with thy mouth the Lord Jesus, and shalt believe in thine heart that God hath raised him from the dead, thou shalt be saved" (Romans 10:9).

www.ingramcontent.com/pod-product-compliance
Lightning Source LLC
Chambersburg PA
CBHW071455040426
42444CB00008B/1345